NEW DIRECTIONS FOR INSTITUTIONAL RESEARCH

J. Fredericks Volkwein, *Penn State University*
EDITOR-IN-CHIEF

Knowledge Management: Building a Competitive Advantage in Higher Education

Andreea M. Serban
Santa Barbara City College

Jing Luan
Cabrillo College

EDITORS

Number 113, Spring 2002

JOSSEY-BASS
A Wiley Company
www.josseybass.com

KNOWLEDGE MANAGEMENT: BUILDING A COMPETITIVE ADVANTAGE IN HIGHER EDUCATION
Andreea M. Serban, Jing Luan (eds.)
New Directions for Institutional Research, no. 113
J. Fredericks Volkwein, Editor-in-Chief

New Directions for Institutional Research is indexed in *College Student Personnel Abstracts, Contents Pages in Education,* and *Current Index to Journals in Education* (ERIC).

Microfilm copies of issues and chapters are available in 16mm and 35mm, as well as microfiche in 105mm, through University Microfilms Inc., 300 North Zeeb Road, Ann Arbor, Michigan 48106-1346.

ISSN 0271-0579   electronic ISSN 1536-075X   ISBN 0-7879-6291-0

NEW DIRECTIONS FOR INSTITUTIONAL RESEARCH is part of The Jossey-Bass Higher and Adult Education Series and is published quarterly by Wiley Subscription Services, Inc., a Wiley company, at Jossey-Bass, 989 Market Street, San Francisco, California 94103-1741 (publication number USPS 098-830). Periodicals postage paid at San Francisco, California, and at additional mailing offices. POSTMASTER: Send address changes to New Directions for Institutional Research, Jossey-Bass, 989 Market Street, San Francisco, California 94103-1741.

SUBSCRIPTIONS cost $65.00 for individuals and $125.00 for institutions, agencies, and libraries.

EDITORIAL CORRESPONDENCE should be sent to J. Fredericks Volkwein, Center for the Study of Higher Education, Penn State University, 400 Rackley Building, University Park, PA 16801-5252.

Photograph of the library by Michael Graves at San Juan Capistrano by Chad Slattery © 1984. All rights reserved.

www.josseybass.com

Printed in the United States of America on acid-free recycled paper containing 100 percent recovered waste paper, of which at least 20 percent is postconsumer waste.

For information about the Association for Institutional Research, write to the following address:

AIR Executive Office
114 Stone Building
Florida State University
Tallahassee, FL 32306-4462

(850) 644-4470

air@mailer.fsu.edu
http://airweb.org

CONTENTS

EDITORS' NOTES

The millennium-old adage "Knowledge is power" has taken a new spin in the era of digitized information. Beginning in the early 1990s, corporations have coined the concept and movement of knowledge management, which is an institutional attempt to capitalize on the cumulative knowledge that an organization has. Definitions of knowledge management vary but two are widely recognized as best capturing the concept:

- "Knowledge management is about connecting people to people and people to information to create competitive advantage" (Knowledge Management News).
- "Knowledge management is the systematic process of identifying, capturing, and transferring information and knowledge people can use to create, compete, and improve" (American Productivity and Quality Center).

The knowledge management paradigm is about transforming data into information into knowledge and ultimately gaining organizational "wisdom" and building competitive advantage. Colleges and universities exist to create and share knowledge. However, few higher education campuses have institutionalized processes that leverage knowledge to spur innovation, improve instructional and support service, or maximize operational efficiency and effectiveness. Whereas knowledge management is not a radically new idea, it is a new way of looking at how higher education institutions could operate more dynamically and effectively in the twenty-first century. Knowledge management is poised to become a mission-critical component.

The purposes of this volume are (1) to discuss the concept of knowledge management, its components and processes, and the role of institutional research in the implementation of knowledge management in higher education and (2) to discuss examples of knowledge management techniques and tools that are best suited for use by institutional researchers. The volume is informative and relevant not only for the work of institutional researchers but also for all administrators, faculty, and information technology staff interested in investigating and implementing a knowledge management approach.

Chapter One provides an overview of knowledge management, including definition, components, processes, and outcomes. It discusses the importance of knowledge management for higher education, in general, and for institutional research, in particular. The chapter serves as the background for the remainder of the volume, which addresses specific examples related to particular components and processes that support knowledge management.

NEW DIRECTIONS FOR INSTITUTIONAL RESEARCH, no. 113, Spring 2002 © Wiley Periodicals, Inc.

Chapter Two discusses data mining, an essential knowledge management process. It examines the theoretical basis for data mining and uses a case study to describe its application and impact.

Chapter Three discusses the concept of portals and its relevance for knowledge management and provides examples of its applicability to higher education organizations and to institutional research. Many businesses have used portals to create personalized profiles and information for each customer or groups of customers. The key premise underlying this approach is that customers want on-demand access to information that is tailored to their needs and preferences. Whereas higher education, in general, has been slow in catching up, some colleges and universities are testing and implementing this mode of operation.

Chapter Four addresses another area that plays an important role within the knowledge management framework—customer relationship management. This is an approach increasingly used by businesses to record, track, and categorize customer information in order to expedite customer follow-up and provide faster and better services. Customer relationship management has direct applicability in the areas of admissions, enrollment management, alumni relations, and fundraising. It is also a valuable tool for institutional researchers as they conduct analyses and studies to inform these processes and functional areas.

The ultimate goal of knowledge management is sharing of knowledge throughout an institution and the creation of learning organizations responsive to change and innovation. Chapter Five discusses organizational learning and the required reassessment and redesign of internal structures and procedures related to the flow of information throughout the organization. It provides a framework for the integration of institutional research within the larger context of organizational learning and the creation and maintenance of a research culture facilitated by knowledge management.

Chapter Six builds on a taxonomy of technologies supporting knowledge management and presents a number of products and vendors representing the various categories in the taxonomy. It also proposes a Tiered Knowledge Management model for institutional research. This model classifies the various types of technologies available to institutional researchers for data gathering, management, retrieval, and analysis. It guides readers through data and information management, system design, required skills, and resource allocation. The chapter provides a roadmap for institutional researchers interested in assessing the feasibility of implementing a knowledge management framework that begins in their offices and possibly extends to their campuses.

The final chapter draws on all the chapters to capture the main themes presented in the volume. Their underlying premise is that the institutional research office could and should play a critical role in advancing the knowledge management paradigm. This concluding chapter looks at the advantages and challenges of knowledge management from an institutional research perspective.

Over time, institutional research has had to reinvent itself repeatedly in response to changes within the internal and external environments that impact its operations and roles. Knowledge management provides exciting opportunities while challenging the organizational and structural status quo. Institutional research is best positioned to take advantage of the opportunities of knowledge management and address its challenges.

Andreea M. Serban
Jing Luan
Editors

ANDREEA M. SERBAN is director of institutional assessment, research, and planning at Santa Barbara City College in Santa Barbara, California.

JING LUAN is chief planning and research officer at Cabrillo College in Aptos, California.

1

Knowledge management is about using the brain power of an organization in a systematic and organized manner in order to achieve efficiencies, ensure competitive advantage, and spur innovation. This chapter discusses the fundamentals of knowledge management, its definitions, components, processes, and relevance for higher education, in general, and institutional research, in particular.

Overview of Knowledge Management

Andreea M. Serban, Jing Luan

In the early 1990s, corporations coined the concept and movement of knowledge management, which is an institutional systematic effort to capitalize on the cumulative knowledge that an organization has. "Knowledge management is a fast-moving field created by the collision of several others, including human resources, organizational development, change management, information technology, brand and reputation management, performance measurement, and evaluation" (Bukowitz and Williams, 1999).

Although a fairly young field, knowledge management has gained tremendous popularity very quickly in the business world. Journals dedicated to this topic include *Knowledge Management Magazine, Knowledge Management Review,* and *Knowledge Management World Magazine.* There are conferences either exclusively dedicated to this field, such as KM World or the Knowledge Management Conferences organized by the American Productivity and Quality Center, or prominently featuring knowledge management both in terms of presentations and vendors, such the annual conferences held by Gartner Research Group and EDUCAUSE. Consulting groups—both well established with a large client base and small, regionally based—have rushed to advertise knowledge management as one of their areas of expertise. Prominent examples include the Gartner Group, the American Productivity and Quality Center, and Klynveld, Peat, Marwick, Goerdeler (KPMG).

Knowledge management presents a significant business opportunity. According to industry expert Ovum (cited in VNU Business Media, 2001), the worldwide knowledge management market will be worth $12.3 billion by the year 2004. More specifically, Ovum forecasts that the worldwide market for knowledge management–related software will increase from $515 million in 1999 to $3.5 billion by 2004. Knowledge management–related services are expected to grow from $2.6 billion in 1999 to $8.8 billion by

NEW DIRECTIONS FOR INSTITUTIONAL RESEARCH, no. 113, Spring 2002 © Wiley Periodicals, Inc.

2004. Among the knowledge management services are those provided by training and performance improvement organizations. Are these impressive figures paralleled by results? A 2001 survey by Reuters finds that 90 percent of companies that deploy a knowledge management solution benefit from better decision making and 81 percent say that they notice increased productivity (Malhotra, 2001). Several reasons account for and technological developments have led to the emergence and growth of this field.

Reasons for Emergence and Growth of Knowledge Management

Reasons for the emergence and growth of this field include the following.

Information Overload and Chaos. Information overwhelms corporations, schools, classrooms, and our minds. Finding what we need to complete a task, especially more complex ones, can be time consuming and frustrating if we do not have access to a well-organized, readily available infrastructure that contains the type of information needed. Information resides in many different sources, some easily accessible, others volatile and highly personal. As Microsoft founder Bill Gates noted in his presentation at COMDEX Fall 1999: "Corporate information today is so hard to find. It's kept in folders, or anecdotally understood by people in the company" (cited in VNU Business Media, 2001). Gates added, "Knowledge workers need to share things, and need access to the right information at the right time. This is so hard today." What is true? Which solution is better? Or what are the solutions? What we have gained are volumes of unfiltered and unprocessed information and what we struggle to find are the time and the ability to respond quickly to ever increasing demands and expectations from our employers and clients, whether they are students or faculty or staff.

Information Congestion. Communication channels bottleneck in our computer networks. We sometimes hear that the Internet access is slow during peak hours at work because too many of us are searching the Web at the same time. Sometimes the speed with which we can tap into available internal data warehouses or transactional operational systems is less than desirable because too many of us are accessing vast amounts of data, thus putting a significant strain on our systems. If we had the mechanisms to target very specifically the data or information we are looking for, the overall speed of our networks would be consistently at its best capacity.

Information and Skill Segmentation and Specialization. The Renaissance era, when a single individual mastered many different domains, is long gone. While there are always exceptions to confirm the rule, most individuals can now master only one domain of expertise and sometimes only segments within one domain. It is often the case that the completion of various projects requires access to and corroboration of information from multiple domains. Having access to the right information, at the right time, without necessarily being an expert in all domains involved, would greatly improve individual and organizational efficiency and effectiveness.

Workforce Mobility and Turnover. The average years an employee spends on one career have been shortened from lifelong to ten and now to three years (United States Department of Labor, 2000). When colleagues retire or change jobs, they take with them valuable experiences and skills for which the institution has paid a premium to search and train. A 2001 survey found that while "26 percent of knowledge in the average organization is stored on paper and 20 percent digitally, an astonishing 42 percent is stored in employees' heads" (Malhotra, 2001). Organizations are increasingly recognizing that capturing and sharing these experiences and skills save them money, prevent or reduce interruptions in activities, and enhance their overall ability to cope with changes in personnel.

Competition. This has always been a main driver for improvement and innovation in the business environment. With the propagation of non-traditional higher education providers and modalities of instructional delivery, such as University of Phoenix and online courses and programs, colleges and universities are increasingly finding themselves competing for students much more than they were accustomed to a decade ago. Being able to anticipate changes in our environments and demands for new programs or courses, and to respond quickly, are becoming prerequisites for how higher education must operate in order to survive, thrive, and adapt to change.

Technological Developments Contributing to Emergence and Growth of Knowledge Management

Whereas knowledge management is not defined by technology, technologies support knowledge management (Hildebrand, 1999; Hayward, 2000). Without the advent of powerful and sophisticated hardware and software tools, the field of knowledge management would have been at most a good subject for theoretical lectures and philosophical exercises. Knowledge management processes perform best when enabled by powerful, yet fairly easy to use once implemented, technologies. As discussed throughout this volume, emphasis on technology alone will achieve little progress toward knowledge management, but even the strongest commitment to knowledge management that is not supported by robust technology will not succeed.

The intersection of the above-mentioned reasons and the fast technological developments of the 1990s has produced an environment conducive to translating the theoretical foundation of knowledge management into practice. Whereas the fact that knowledge is power is as old as the human civilization, having the means to put in place organizationwide systems that constantly and systematically capture and capitalize on this power is a fairly recent, evolving capability.

In finding ways to work with knowledge as an asset, organizations are transforming knowledge from an abstract concept to an increasingly tangible and manageable one. This transformation has spawned new concepts and terminology, thereby strengthening the relationship between information and technology, as well as developing new processes and approaches to designing information resources and new cultures (VNU Business Media, 2001). The remainder of this chapter is dedicated to describing these concepts, terminology, processes, and cultures and their applicability to higher education in general and institutional research in particular.

What Is Knowledge?

Epistemology is the study of the nature and grounds of knowledge. Epistemologists reason that knowledge is "justified belief." They contemplate the eternal challenge of separating true from false. As Nonaka and Takeuchi (1995) point out: "we consider knowledge as a dynamic human process of justifying personal belief toward the 'truth.'" There has been a lineage of this branch of philosophy that recognized knowledge as awareness of absolute and permanent facts. Kantian synthesis, a branch of rationalism and empiricism, later developed the notion that knowledge came from the organization of perceptual data on the basis of categories, including space, time, objects, and causality. Their theory moved from Plato's view to the subjectivity of basic concepts about space and time. At the turn of the century, a subbranch called pragmatism, an American movement in philosophy founded by C. S. Peirce and William James, extended its definition of knowledge as a result of the influence of artificial intelligence and quantum mechanics. It stated that knowledge consists of "models," which reflect the surrounding environment, resulting in targeted, simplified problem-solving and cognitive conclusions. The evolution (not to be confused with evolutionary epistemology) of epistemology resembles the modern recognition of the knowledge creation hierarchy: data to information to knowledge as represented in Figure 1.1.

Plato's view of absolute and permanent attributes of knowledge is the equivalent of the starting point of knowledge: data. Data are building blocks that are unitary, independent, and timeless. Data are raw facts and numbers, which can be informative but by themselves provide little value for decision making, planning, or any other action. Data gain meaning once they are put into context (Kidwell, Vander Linde, and Johnson, 2000) and once the relations between data and context are understood. "[When] endowed with relevance and purpose," as Drucker (1999) stated, data become information. Davenport and Prusak (1998) listed the following values added by the transformation of data into information: contextualization, categorization, calculation, correction, and condensement.

Knowledge combines information with individual, group, and organizational experience and judgment, and it involves making a leap from

Figure 1.1. From Data to Knowledge

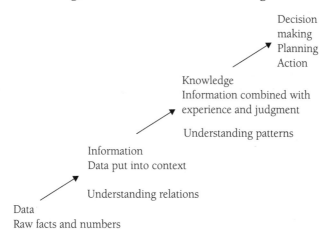

understanding relations to understanding patterns that can guide action. Or as O'Dell, Essaides, and Ostro (1998) describe, "knowledge is information in action." Davenport and Prusak (1998) point to the following processes involved in the transformation of information into knowledge: comparison, consequence, connection, and conversation.

Explicit Versus Tacit Knowledge

Knowledge takes various forms. Edvinson and Malone (1997), both organizational experts, categorize knowledge into individual, structural, and organizational. They regard structural knowledge as what has been codified into manuals and reports and organizational knowledge the activity of learning within the organization. Structural knowledge builds on data available in databases and data warehouses and on the other fluid, intangible, personalized entities that exist only in biological human brains. Modern philosopher and chemist Polanyi (1964, 1974, 1983) and practitioners Nonaka and Takeuchi (1995) have, at different times, reasoned that structured or codified building blocks are explicit knowledge whereas unstructured, difficult-to-codify building blocks are tacit knowledge. Crowley (2000) echoed that explicit knowledge, as codified knowledge, is transmittable in formal, systematic language; and tacit knowledge is personal, context-specific, and difficult to formalize and codify. Tacit knowledge is personal in origin, job specific, related to context, difficult to fully articulate, and poorly documented but highly operational in the minds of the possessor (Kidwell, Vander Linde, and Johnson, 2000). Table 1.1 summarizes the features and sources of explicit and tacit knowledge.

Knowledge management is, then, the systematic and organized approach of organizations to manipulate and take advantage of both explicit

Table 1.1. Explicit Versus Tacit Knowledge

	Explicit Knowledge (Documented)	Tacit Knowledge (Know-how embedded in people)
Features	Easily codified Storable Transferable Easily expressed and shared	Personal Context-specific Difficult to formalize Difficult to capture, communicate, share
Sources	Manuals Policies and procedures Databases and reports	Informal business processes and communications Personal experiences Historical understanding

and tacit knowledge, which in turn leads to the creation of new knowledge. Or as the American Productivity and Quality Center summarizes: "Knowledge Management is the systematic process of identifying, capturing, and transferring information and knowledge people can use to create, compete, and improve." These activities are not entirely discrete, but they cause a different focus on processes, tools, techniques, and the individuals or groups to whom they are addressed (Hayward, 2000). These aspects are discussed in the next section of the chapter and are further exemplified by the other chapters in the volume.

Sources of Knowledge

Davenport and Prusak (1998) suggest five types of knowledge that correspond to the source of each.

• *Acquired knowledge* comes from outside the organization. In some cases, an organization purchases the knowledge from another source. Similarly, information can be leased or rented. For example, some "rented" knowledge comes from consultants. Institutional research relies heavily on rented knowledge such as U.S. Census Data, Integrated Postsecondary Education Data System (IPEDS) files, research methods, to name a few. Davenport and Prusak note that "originality is less important than usefulness" in acquired knowledge.

• *Dedicated resources* are those in which an organization sets aside some staff members or an entire department (usually research and development) to develop within the institution for a specific purpose. These dedicated resources are usually protected from competitive pressures to develop profitable products. Offices of institutional research are by themselves good examples of dedicated resources to the extent that they generally serve specific purposes, which are not duplicated or shared by other departments and offices. This is particularly true when institutional research functions are centralized within one office.

• *Fusion* is knowledge created by bringing together people with different perspectives to work on the same project. The resulting projects represent more comprehensive expertise than possible if members of the team represented one perspective. But Davenport and Prusak note that fused knowledge often involves conflict, and a team needs time to reach a shared knowledge and language. Cross-functional teams are becoming popular in higher education institutions and are examples of fusion. Institutional researchers are often called upon to participate in various teams due to their expertise.

• *Adaptation* is knowledge that results from responding to new processes or technologies in the market place. The expansion of on-line instruction offered by higher education institutions is an example of adaptation.

• *Knowledge networking* is knowledge in which people share information with one another formally or informally. Knowledge networking often occurs within disciplines; for example, an institutional researcher communicating with another.

Knowledge Management: Taxonomy, Processes, and Components

Knowledge management involves a number of iterative processes, some of which are intertwined and could occur simultaneously. The premise of these processes is that knowledge management implies continuous and ongoing renewal of organizational schemas to anticipate future opportunities and threats (Malhotra, 1998). These processes "link people and knowledge content" (Hayward, 2000) and are summarized in Figure 1.2.

At the core of the knowledge management framework is the creation of knowledge. All organizations, higher education institutions, in particular, create knowledge. Creation of knowledge can occur through a variety

Figure 1.2. Knowledge Management Processes

Knowledge Content

Knowledge Management Processes				
Create	**Capture**	**Organize**	**Access**	**Use**
• Discover	• Digitize	• Structure	• Present	• Make
• Realize	• Document	• Catalog	• Display	• Improve
• Conclude	• Extract	• Abstract	• Notify	• Perform
• Articulate	• Represent	• Analyze	• Profile	• Service
• Discuss	• Store	• Categorize	• Find	• Learn

Collaborate   Find   Mediate   Facilitate   Augment   Share   Align

People Processes

Source: Gartner Research, in Hayward (2000). Reproduced with permission of Gartner Group.

of means, such as scientific discovery or discussions. However, knowledge can be easily lost or not used if it is not captured. From a technological perspective, capturing knowledge can be achieved through digitization, documentation, extraction, representation, and storage. There are numerous techniques and software tools available for each of these methods, and they are addressed in Chapter Six.

Far more important in the process of knowledge management is knowledge sharing. The tacit knowledge possessed by individuals is crucial and instrumental to an organization's operation and survival. However, reaching the point where employees willingly share what they know "is one of the toughest nuts organizations have to crack" (Bukowitz and Williams, 1999). Technology has made it relatively easy to organize, post, and transfer certain types of information. "On the other hand, contribution is not only time consuming, but is also seen as a threat to individual employee viability" (Bukowitz and Williams, 1999). Unless the organizational environment rewards knowledge sharing, the entire effort to institutionalize a knowledge management system will falter. These aspects are discussed in more detail in Chapter Five.

Collaboration is another key process that should permeate the organizational knowledge management approach. What organization does not have task forces, committees, project teams, or work groups? The manner in which a modern organization is governed, the way curricula are determined, and the statements written in institutional policies all inexplicitly involve the expectation that individuals work collaboratively. Groupware activities, including sharing of calendars, collective writing, e-mail handling, shared database access, electronic meetings with each person able to see and display information to others, among others, contribute to facilitating virtual and easy collaboration.

To share the knowledge is not nearly the end of knowledge management. What often fails in knowledge management is the inability to shepherd the entire process. Szulanksi (1994) found four barriers to successful sharing and transferring of knowledge: ignorance on both ends of the transfer, absorptive capacity, lack of relationship between the giver and receiver, and slow rate of adoption. Many corporations have tuned in to these four barriers. These potential hidden obstacles hampering knowledge management have been widely recognized by corporations. Another painful truth is that even though some organizations have been managing knowledge in one form or another, they have not organized the knowledge in a meaningful fashion. Therefore, organizations and employees have been struggling with a convoluted potpourri of data, information, and knowledge without specific mechanisms to leverage their power. Organizing knowledge in a meaningful taxonomy is a challenging task, especially in large organizations with many different individual and group needs. At the same time, the access to knowledge must be relatively easy. A well-thought-out taxonomy would definitely facilitate the ease of access as would notification mechanisms and personalization of information. As described in Chapter Three, well-developed portals can address most of these concerns and processes.

Finally, the ultimate test of any knowledge management system is its use. The best-built portal structure will have little value if the employees do not use it. Some institutional researchers may have experienced the frustration of developing and deploying decision support systems only to find themselves providing the same reports that one could easily obtain from available systems. As with any new endeavor, resistance to change is one of the barriers to successful implementation of knowledge management systems. However, if the perceived (and actual) benefits of such systems are greater than the perceived effort to learn a new tool or adopt a new model of operation, then the chances of success are very high.

Relevance of Knowledge Management for Higher Education and Institutional Research

In many institutions of higher education, there is no organized knowledge management system in place or even an understanding of such a system (Kidwell, Vander Linde, and Johnson, 2000). Since higher education is about the creation, transformation, and transmission of knowledge (Laudon and Laudon, 1999), such an oversight is striking. However, some colleges and universities are making good progress in this direction, as described in the following chapters.

Kidwell, Vander Linde, and Johnson (2000) are among those who conceptualized the potential applications and benefits of knowledge management for higher education. In the area of faculty, student, and curriculum development, for example, they advocated for portal-based access to a repository of pedagogy and assessment techniques, student evaluations, and curriculum revision efforts. Benefits of such access could range from enhanced quality of curriculum and programs to improved responsiveness in incorporating ideas from best practices to improved administrative intervention. For research-related knowledge management, they envisioned a repository or a portal for research outcomes, preformatted proposals and budget forms, as well as overview of internal services, resources, and staff. The benefit could be less redundancy and expedited research applications that leverage existing research efforts. They also detailed knowledge management applications for administrative services and strategic planning. Chapter Three provides a detailed discussion of the features and advantages of portal technologies for higher education institutions and exemplifies how a college has put into practice some of the conceptual models proposed by these authors.

Whereas Chapter Three focuses primarily on internal knowledge management, Chapter Four discusses customer relationship management

(CRM), an aggressive and mission critical knowledge management tool that provides institutions with the framework and technology needed for tracking and communicating with their clients, including prospective and current students and their parents and alumni. CRM puts organizational knowledge to the test by facilitating real-time interaction between customers and the service provider. CRM recognizes relationships as the key components in organizational operations. Relationships exist everywhere in higher education. The most important relationship is between faculty and students. Higher education as an entity for knowledge creation and transfer can learn from CRM by focusing on the relationship between students (the learners) and the college (the knowledge provider). Our learners have become more demanding, their needs more diverse, and they are more vocal in expressing their wishes. Colleges cannot survive by simply opening the door and waiting for students to walk in to enroll. If you build it, they may *not* come.

Von Holzen (2000) stated that new education models will soon emerge. Sullivan (2001) went a step further to indicate the possibility of current education providers being replaced by for-profit entities should they be slow to change. Currently, growth-oriented institutions are focusing on enrollment management. Whereas this is an important area, it will not be entirely effective by itself, perhaps because it tends to make the admissions office the focal point but leaves out everything else that a learner experiences, receives, and interacts with in their "whole experience." Instead of thinking of managing enrollment, the focus might be better placed on managing the relationship between the learner and the college or university. One direction to take is to expand the notion of enrollment management or collapse many existing enrollment projects under the notion of "learner relationship management" (LRM) (Luan, 2001). Just like the paradigm shift from teaching to learning, the shift from narrowly focused enrollment management to learner relationship management is profound. The theories of learning and the notion of accountability notwithstanding, the entire process of providing learning is, first of all, a relationship. Learner relationship management will prompt the college or university to proactively examine a whole suite of issues, factors, information, and knowledge related to the various relationships centering on the needs of learners. Identifying and satisfying the needs of learners are among the most effective means to handle enrollment, retention, marketing, student success, and a host of accountability related issues, henceforth, *knowledge management*.

Institutional research is an empirical example of how explicit knowledge management applies. Institutional research relies primarily on two sources: explicit data and existing literature. Data are either from data warehouses or quantitative or qualitative information obtained from surveys, interviews, and focus groups. Research literature typically refers to learned experiences and tried methodologies. Researchers either develop a new methodology or replicate what already exists. Institutional research has always intuitively followed the process of transforming data into information and further into knowledge. The textbook description of a researcher has always been one who frames a research question, reviews the literature, identifies a sample of data, develops a hypothesis, tests the hypothesis, and writes up the findings. Some may go further to provide policy recommendations. Most of what researchers perform today still fits this scenario, but with heightened intensity, speed, and skills.

The institutional research field is under constant change in the area of explicit knowledge enhanced by technologies. From a data management perspective, the data warehousing industry has expanded dramatically over the last two decades. It is a fast-developing enterprise that has left the confines of a few privileged corporations (mainly those who could afford it) to be widely available for implementation. It is not rare to see data warehouses with terabytes of data at some American universities. Data mining, discussed in detail in the next chapter, has pushed the envelope further by linking sophisticated pattern recognition through direct communication with a data warehouse deployed over the Web. The Internet has fundamentally changed the way we display information or access data. Printed hard copies of reports have given way to on-line real-time query results, or soft copies. The Internet will drive software, not the other way around. A significant amount of a researcher's time is in the area of designing and maintaining reports for decision making. Researchers have to split their time between data warehousing and querying and, in the near future, among data mining, building and maintaining portals, and managing documents and contents.

References

American Productivity and Quality Center. [http://www.apqc.org/km/].

Bukowitz, W. R., and Williams, R. L. *The Knowledge Management Fieldbook.* Upper Saddle River, N.J.: Financial Times, Prentice Hall, 1999.

Crowley, B. "Knowledge Management for the Information Professional." In K. Srikantaiah and M. Koenig (eds.), *Tacit Knowledge and Quality Assurance: Bridging the Theory-Practice Divide.* Medford, N.J.: Informational Today Inc., 2000.

Davenport, T., and Prusak, L. *Working Knowledge: How Organizations Manage What They Know.* Boston: Harvard Business School Press, 1998.

Drucker, P. F. *Management Challenges for the 21st Century.* New York: HarperBusiness, 1999.

Edvinson, L., and Malone, M. *Intellectual Capital.* New York: HarperCollins, 1997.

Hayward, S. "Choosing Wisely: Technology for Knowledge Management." Paper presented at the Gartner Symposium ITXPO, Orlando, Fla., Oct. 16–20, 2000.

Hildebrand, C. "Does KM = IT?" *CIO Enterprise Magazine,* Sept. 15, 1999. [http://www.cio.com/archive/enterprise/091599_ic_content.html].

Kidwell, J. J., Vander Linde, K. M., and Johnson, S. L. "Applying Corporate Knowledge Management Practices in Higher Education." *EDUCAUSE Quarterly,* 2000, 4, 28–33.

Knowledge Management Magazine. [http://www.destinationcrm.com/km/dcrm_km_index.asp].

Knowledge Management Review. [http://www.km-review.com/].

Knowledge Management World Magazine. [http://www.kmworld.com/].

Laudon, K., and Laudon, J. *Management Information Systems-Organization and Technology in the Networked Enterprise.* Englewood Cliffs, N.J.: Prentice Hall, 1999.

Luan, J. "Learner Relationship Management: Signs of Things to Come." Paper presented at the Annual Conference of the Community College League of California, Riverside, Calif., 2001.

Malhotra, Y. "Knowledge Management, Knowledge Organizations and Knowledge Workers: A View from the Front Lines." 1998 [http://www.brint.com/interview/maeil.htm].

Malhotra, Y. "It's Time to Cultivate Growth." *Leading Views,* March, 2001. [http://www.youcan.bt.com/youcan/flash/lw/mar2001/cultivate_growth.html].

Nonaka, I., and Takeuchi, H. *The Knowledge-Creating Company: How Japanese Companies Create the Dynamics of Innovation.* London: Oxford University Press, 1995.

O'Dell, C. S., Essaides, N., and Ostro, N. *If Only We Knew What We Know: The Transfer of Internal Knowledge and Best Practice.* Detroit: Free Press, 1998.

Polanyi, M. *Science, Faith, and Society.* Chicago: University of Chicago Press, 1964.

Polanyi, M. *Personal Knowledge Towards a Post-Critical Philosophy.* Chicago: University of Chicago Press, 1974.

Polanyi, M. *Tacit Dimension.* London: Peter Smith Publications, 1983.

Sullivan, R. S. "Science, Technology, and Innovation Policy: Opportunities and Challenges for the Knowledge Economy." In P. Conceicao, D. Gibson, M. Heiter, et al. (eds.), *Science, Technology, and Innovation Policy: Opportunities and Challenges for the Knowledge Economy.* Westport: Quorum Books, 2001.

Szulanksi, G. *Intra-Firm Transfer of Best Practices Project.* Houston: American Productivity and Quality Center, 1994.

United States Department of Labor. "Employee Tenure Summary." Aug., 2000. [http://www.bls.gov/news.release/tenure.nr0.htm].

VNU Business Media. "Eight Things That Training and Performance Improvement Professionals Must Know About Knowledge Management." 2001 [http://www.destinationcrm.com/km/dcrm_km_article.asp?id=934].

Von Holzen, R. "A Look at the Future of Higher Education." *Syllabus,* November, 2000.

ANDREEA M. SERBAN is director of institutional assessment, research, and planning at Santa Barbara City College in Santa Barbara, California.

JING LUAN is chief planning and research officer at Cabrillo College in Aptos, California.

2

Data mining is the process of discovering "hidden messages," patterns and knowledge within large amounts of data and of making predictions for outcomes or behaviors. This chapter discusses in detail the theoretical and practical aspects of data mining and provides a case study of its application to college transfer data.

Data Mining and Its Applications in Higher Education

Jing Luan

The first chapter has afforded readers an opportunity to review the definitions and components of knowledge management. The chapter also established that knowledge management is closely linked to technology. Explicit knowledge, which is a product of several major technologies, is the focus of this chapter. Specifically, this chapter addresses data mining.

One among a host of recent technology innovations, data mining is making changes to the entire makeup of our skills and comfort zones in information analysis. Not only does it introduce an array of new concepts, methods, and phrases, it also departs from the well-established, traditional, hypothesis-based statistical techniques. Data mining is a new type of exploratory and predictive data analysis whose purpose is to delineate systematic relations between variables when there are no (or incomplete) *a priori* expectations as to the nature of those relations.

Herman Hollerith's invention of punch cards in 1880 and of a counting machine for the 1890 census led to the development of modern data management and computing techniques. Thearling (1995) even chronicled the evolution of data as *data collection* in the 1960s, *data access* in the 1980s, *data navigation* in the 1990s, and *data mining* in the new century. Thearling (1995) and others foresaw the possibilities of data mining as a result of maturity of all three disciplines: massive data collection and storage, powerful multiprocessor computers, and data mining algorithms. According to Rubenking (2001), "data mining is a logical evolution in database technology. The earliest databases, which served as simple replacements for paper records, were data repositories that provided little more than the capability to summarize and report. With the development of query tools such as SQL

[Structured Query Language], database managers were able to query data more flexibly."

In summary, data mining is possible due to

- Storage and computing power
- Database technology
- Integrated and maturing data mining techniques
- Strong need for fast, vast, and production-driven outcome
- Learner relationship management

Learner relationship management, discussed in the opening chapter, acts as an agent for moving fast on data mining. Higher education is transitioning from the enrollment mode to recruitment mode (Roueche and Roueche, 2000). Higher education institutions find that they cannot continue to operate in the "receive and process" mode. Instead, they must actively seek prospective students. They must cater to students' needs instead of designing a program with the attitude of "take it or leave it." This transition alone will exert great pressure for finding ways to make recruitment more efficient and institutions more attuned to learners' needs. Last, but not least, is the notion of accountability to which higher education can better respond with more powerful tools.

What Is Data Mining?

Artificial intelligence and artificial neural networks, along with almost all data mining techniques, were the brainchild of scholars in higher education, but data mining was not first applied to higher education. Suffice it to say that higher education is still virgin territory for data mining. The amount of data produced in higher education alone calls for some serious data mining. With institutions adopting Enterprise Resource Planning applications, such as Peoplesoft, Datatel, or SAP, kilobytes of data are being created and stored every hour when school is in session. Built for handling extremely large datasets, data mining has enjoyed tremendous growth in the corporate world and several government agencies, such as the FBI. The benefits range from finding hidden patterns in the customer mix, outliers in fraud detection, and targeted product promotion, to name just a few.

Data mining is an evolving field with new concepts born monthly and current concepts struggling to retain their place. Many of the new and interdisciplinary concepts, such as the stochastic search methods (including genetic algorithms), market basket analysis, memory based reasoning, and Bayesian averages, were not even imagined less than a decade ago. Researchers from different branches of mathematics, statistics, marketing, or artificial intelligence will use different terminologies. Where a statistician sees dependent and independent variables, and an artificial intelligence researcher sees features and attributes, others see records and fields (Berry and Linoff, 1997). The phrase "neural networks" is synonymous with data mining.

Although data mining is known for having exotic names, the field has begun to include certain kinds of descriptive statistics and visualization techniques into data mining (Westphal and Blaxton, 1998). Statsoft, an on-line statistical software provider, seemed to favor "exploratory data analysis." Berthold and Hand (1999) called their work "intelligent data analysis." This chapter will refer to all activities involving modeling and nonhypothesis-based analytical techniques as data mining and adopt the concept developed by Berthold and Hand that all statistical techniques developed prior to the 1960s are "classic" and "conformatory."

The definition of data mining from Gartner Group seems to be most comprehensive: "the process of discovering meaningful new correlations, patterns, and trends by sifting through large amounts of data stored in repositories and by using pattern recognition technologies as well as statistical and mathematical techniques" (Gartner Group, 2000). I refine the notion of data mining as the purpose of uncovering hidden trends and patterns and making accuracy based predictions through higher levels of analytical sophistication. It is producing new observations from existing observations. As explained by Rubenking (2001), "data mining is the process of automatically extracting useful information and relationships from immense quantities of data. In its purest form, data mining doesn't involve looking for specific information. Rather than starting from a question or a hypothesis, data mining simply finds patterns that are already present in the data."

Finally, in statistical language, Statsoft (2001) categorizes typical on-line analytical processing (OLAP) techniques as basic statistical exploratory methods or exploratory data analysis that include such techniques as "examining distributions of variables (e.g., to identify highly skewed or non-normal, such as bi-modal patterns), reviewing large correlation matrices for coefficients that meet certain thresholds, or examining multi-way frequency tables (e.g., 'slice by slice' systematically reviewing combinations of levels of control variables)." It reserves the term "multivariate exploratory techniques" for data mining. These techniques are designed specifically to identify patterns in multivariate (or univariate, such as sequences of measurements) data sets that include cluster analysis, factor analysis, discriminant function analysis, multidimensional scaling, log-linear analysis, canonical correlation, stepwise linear and nonlinear (for example, logit) regression, correspondence analysis, time series analysis, and classification trees.

Essential Concepts and Definitions

Data mining assumes the existence of spherical multi-Euclidean dimensions (Delmater and Hancock, 2001). The n-dimensional Euclidean space, or Euclidean hyperspace, is called feature space, where any given coordinates of ordered triples or ordered pairs are viewed as feature vectors. The understanding of Gaussian distribution, z-scores, and regression equations is very useful in data mining. One of the fundamental concepts operating within the data mining hyperspace is the cluster, which is formed of sets of feature vectors that are understood by examining their standard deviations. The tighter the vectors cluster, the better it is for classification purposes. In this case, the clusters are considered as good features, or gestalts.

Both rule induction and neural network data mining techniques fall under the category of machine learning (Hand, 1999), and they are based on various sophisticated and high-speed modeling techniques for predicting outcomes or uncovering hidden patterns. Tools for data mining are constantly emerging, and there are perhaps as many vendors of data mining software as data mining techniques. Some examples of data mining products and vendors are provided in Chapter Six. Frequently cited and used tools such as C&RT (classification and regression trees) and CHAID (chi-squared automatic induction), artificial neural networks (ANN), K-means, nearest neighbor, MBA (market basket analysis), MBR (memory based reasoning), automatic cluster detection, link analysis, decision trees, and genetic algorithms are most familiar to the data mining community.

Data mining is further divided into supervised and unsupervised knowledge discovery. Unsupervised knowledge discovery is to recognize relationships in the data and supervised knowledge discovery is to explain those relationships once they have been found (Berry and Linoff, 1997; Thearling, 1995; Westphal and Blaxton, 1998). Berry and Linoff (1997) described unsupervised knowledge discovery as a bottom-up approach that makes no prior assumptions; the data are allowed to speak for themselves.

To begin to better understand how data mining can be of use to institutional researchers is to examine the tasks performed and the tools used. Data mining tasks are categorized as follows: classification, estimation, segmentation, and description. Table 2.1 lists the tasks and the corresponding tools.

Table 2.1. Classification of Data Mining Tasks and Tools

Tasks	Supervised	Unsupervised
Classification	Memory based reasoning, genetic algorithm, C&RT, link analysis, C5.0, ANN	Kohonen nets
Estimation	ANN, C&RT	—
Segmentation[a]	Market basket analysis, memory based reasoning, link analysis, rule induction	Cluster detection, K-means, generalized rule induction, APRIORI
Description	Rule induction, market basket analysis	Spatial visualization

[a]For ease of understanding, the author includes tasks of affinity grouping, association, and clustering in Segmentation.

The main goal of a classification task is using data mining models to label output that is defined as a category of good-bad or yes-no. According to Berry and Linoff (2000), the estimation tasks refer to data mining models with outputs that are likelihood functions, or even more directly, sizes or length. Classification also functions for filling in missing values (data imputing). Segmentation includes tasks of affinity grouping and association, and clustering. Description has surpassed conventional visualization of a final outcome of data mining. Techniques or models used for descriptions are applicable to data modeling process in its entirety.

Cluster detection is inherently unsupervised data mining (Berry and Linoff, 1997) and decision trees are used for supervised data mining. C&RT and CHAID fall under this class. Genetic algorithms are similar to statistics, in that the form of the model needs to be known in advance. Genetic algorithms use the selection, crossover, and mutation operators to evolve successive generation of solutions. As the generations evolve, only the most predictive survive, until the functions converge on an optimal solution. When the inputs have many categorical variables, decision trees often work well. When the relationship between the inputs and the output is difficult to figure out, neural networks are frequently the technique of choice (Berry and Linoff, 1997).

Neural networks work best when the nature of the data is nonlinear. Running neural networks may take a very long time due to back-propagating. Most neural networks rely on the process for the hidden layer to perform the summation and constantly adjust the weights until it reaches an optimal threshold, which then produces the outcome for a record (Garson, 1998). However, if the researcher terminates an active neural network at any given time while it is being trained on a test dataset, it will still provide useful results. Everything else being equal, fewer inputs will shorten the training time. Some in the data mining community advocate the use of decision trees before neural networks. Others prefer comparing both types of models simultaneously to see which one produces the most accurate model. The latter technique is called "bagging."

This chapter focuses on decision trees, also called rule induction technique, and back-propagation neural networks, a frequently used artificial neural network (ANN). These are also the tools selected in the case study presented later in the chapter.

Decision Trees (CART and C5.0). Decision trees, also called rule induction techniques, are fairly easy to explain, since the notions of trees, leaves, and splits are generally understood. Inductive reasoning refers to estimation of a sample while the population is known. Decision trees use splits to conduct modeling and produce rule sets. For instance, a simple rule set might say

If financial aid = "Yes", and high school GPA $\geq$ 3.0 and
If university GPA $\geq$ 3.5, then persistence = *yes* (confidence = 0.87)
(*sub-rules suppressed . . .*)

Figure 2.1. Diagram of a Decision Tree

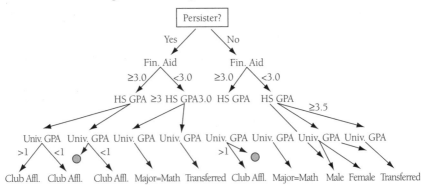

If high school GPA < 3.0 and major = "math", and
If club affiliation < 1, then persistence = *no* (confidence = 0.90)
(*sub-rules suppressed . . .*)
  . . .

Heuristic based decision trees, also called rule induction techniques, include classification and regression trees (C&RT) as well as C5.0. C&RT handles binary splits best, whereas multiple splits are best taken by C5.0. If a tree has only two-way splits, it is considered a binary tree, otherwise a ternary tree. For most of their applications, decision trees start the split from the root (root node) into leave nodes, but on occasion they reverse the course to move from the leaves back to the root. Figure 2.1 is a graphical rendition of a decision tree (binary).

The algorithms differ in the criterion used to drive the splitting. C5.0 relies on measures in the realm of the Information Theorem and C&RT uses the Gini coefficient (SPSS, 2000). Rule induction is fundamentally a task of reducing the uncertainty (entropy) by assigning data into partitions within the feature space based on information-theoretic approaches (van den Eijkel, 1999). The mathematical formula on discerning uncertainty is expressed as measurements in bits:

$$H(N) = \sum_{n=1}^{n} - P(n) \log_2 P(n)$$

where H(N) is the uncertainty defined as discrete information and $P(n)$ is the probability that $\epsilon = n$. As uncertainty reduces, bits are reduced. Suppose the issue is a decision on yes versus no, the conditional information H ($N|yes$) is expressed as follows:

$$H(N|yes) = \sum_{n=1}^{n} - P(n|yes) \log_2 P(n|yes)$$

As with any artificial intelligence, algorithms tend to continue indefinitely once executed (Garson, 1998). As in developing rule sets, decision trees may split into fine leaf nodes that render themselves incapable of predicting, because no future records will be similar at such a fine level of splitting. This is considered to be underfitting. However, overfitting, a trade-off between bias and variance, is also a concern in using these techniques. The method to control the extent to which the tree splits is called pruning. Short trees tend to have higher bias. If the leaf node is not completely developed, or the tree is pruned too soon, then most anything will look alike to the model. A case befitting this scenario would be stopping the split at the node level of the first occurrence of gender. The model may determine that the rest of the relationships within or between the records will not be examined. In this case, a student may be predicted to be successful no matter what he or she does, so long as the student's gender is female or male. At some point, the development of leaf nodes needs to stop. One school of thought in handling the degree with which a tree is considered properly pruned is Occam's razor, which states a simpler explanation is more likely to capture the essence of the problem (van den Eijkel, 1999). Only humans can intuitively make that decision. This reason alone is why humans most certainly cannot be replaced completely by any or a combination of all the data mining algorithms.

Chi-Squared Automatic Induction (CHAID). CHAID was developed by J. A. Hartigan, who borrowed an earlier work by J. A. Morgan and J. N. Sonquest in automatic induction detection (AID). CHAID limits itself to categorical variables. Continuous variables need to be changed into ranges or classes. However, one benefit of CHAID is its ability to stop the split before overfitting occurs.

Artificial Neural Networks (ANN). Our brain has 10^9 neurons interconnected in a complex way. There can be several thousand connections per neuron, potentially amounting to 60 trillion synapses (Garson, 1998). The precise manner of how neurons, or the inner layer of these neural networks, operate remains unknown (Brieman, 1994). The artificial intelligence developed in the 1960s underwent tremendous modification to better mimic the inner functions of the brain. The current theory is a revisit to the Pavlovian theory, further advanced by renowned neurological system scientist Donald Hebb, who theorized that learning is a result of the strength of the synaptic connections, rather than the older concept that learning is a result of manipulations of symbols (Statsoft, 2001).

Developed as a mathematical rendition to explain the function of the nervous system by neurophysiologist Warren McCulloch and logician

Walter Pitts, their concept of an artificial neural net composed of binary-valued neurons opened a brand new chapter in data analysis. Their mathematical model, as a step function, mimics the way nerve cells process information either for excitatory synapse or inhibitory synapse or for enhancing and reducing the transmitted signal (Silipo, 1999). Although biological neurons are inherently analog in nature, the artificial neuron by McCulloch and Pitts can perform Boolean operations (Not, Or, and And) with the proper adjustment of weights and threshold at which a perceptron would produce an output (called neuron firing). All contemporary neural networks bear the imprints of the McCulloch-Pitts model. The field of neural networks almost suffered irreparable failure in the late 1960s due to the discovery of its inability to model the Boolean operation of exclusive-OR (XOR) by two researchers at MIT. It was not until the 1980s, when John Hopfield invented the back-propagation method (sometimes called error back propagation), that interest in ANN was rekindled. The networks feed back through the network errors discovered in prediction, modifying the weights by a small amount each time, until all example records have been processed, perhaps many times, while discarding unneeded inputs (Watkins, 2000). With the advent of computing technology, ANN flourishes today.

Figure 2.2 presents an example of a multilayer perceptron (MLP) of an ANN with two outputs, which is used in the case study presented later in this chapter.

Several authors have described mathematically the formulae for back-propagating neural networks (Hand, 1999). In a book helpful for institutional researchers, *Neural Networks: an Introductory Guide for Social Scientists,*

Figure 2.2. Diagram of the Case Study Neural Net

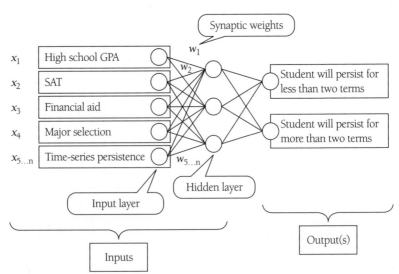

Garson (1998) treated the inner workings of an MLP as a weighted summation function and a sigmoid transfer function. He explained the process of dendrites (inputs) passing information to reach a threshold for axons (output) to signal the connected neural nets using the mathematical formulae

$$o_j = f\left(\sum_{i=1}^{n} o_i w_{ji}\right), \text{ where } f'(x) = -(1 + e^{-x})^{-2} e^{-x}(-1)$$

where o is the outcome, x_i is the input vector, w_i is the weight, which is set at random upon first feed.

Kohonen Neural Networks. There are many alternative neural networks. One of the most well known is the Kohonen neural network. Developed by Finnish researcher Tuevo Kohonen, Kohonen neural networks primarily act as an unsupervised knowledge discovery technique. Garson (1998) stated that Kohonen nets are estimators of the probability density function for the input vector. Some data miners call it self-organizing maps (SOM), which means intuitively that the outcome is a result of allowing the algorithms to analyze the variables until certain patterns emerge (Berry and Linoff, 2000; Silipo, 1999). In formulaic terms,

$$d_j = \sqrt{\left[\sum_{i=1}^{n} (x_{ji} - w_{ji})^2\right]}$$

where the Euclidean distance d of neuron j is the sum of the squared distances from x (inputs) and the assigned weights of x.

Kohonen nets are useful for discerning patterns and groups within a feature space. Researchers may use Kohonen nets to learn about the data before building other models. They have great value in understanding who takes what clusters of courses or what groups of students tend to have similar course-taking patterns.

Statistics, Data Mining, and On-Line Analytical Processing

Delmater and Hancock (2001, p. 192) wrote: "The science underlying predictive modeling is a mixture of mathematics, computer science, and domain expertise." Their point is very well taken and is the focus of this section. Data mining is a knowledge discovery process to reveal patterns and relationships in large and complex data sets (De Veaux, 2000). Moreover, data mining can be used to predict an outcome for a given entity. The ultimate reason for carrying out pattern identification or rule setting is to use the knowledge gained from this exercise to influence the policy makers.

Most of the processes involved in data mining are explainable by mathematics, statistics in particular, and are to a certain extent familiar to researchers who are comfortable with explication statistics. Even in the so-called "data fishing expedition" of conducting unsupervised data mining, the algorithms are still based on logics and formulae.

Table 2.2, which I developed, provides a crosswalk comparison among the major concepts in data mining, statistics, and on-line analytical processing (OLAP). A crosswalk like this provides a guide for understanding data mining terminologies and concepts. It is not intended, however, to be all-inclusive, as researchers can spend a lifetime collecting and categorizing the ever-growing data mining models (Garson, 1998) and terminologies.

In the early days of computing when classical statistics were the only tools of choice, reducing data size was crucial (Berry and Linoff, 1997). The power delivered by data warehousing to data mining software has challenged traditional statistical methodologies (Mena, 1998). Rather than approaching a problem in a limited source domain that typically is a sample of data identified by the guidance of *a priori* hypotheses, researchers can now overlay data mining algorithms on the entire population. This entire

Table 2.2. Crosswalk of Data Mining Models and Algorithms to Statistics and Data Warehouse Based OLAP

Data Mining	Statistics	Data Warehousing, OLAP
Artificial neural networks	Regression equations, chi-square, structural equations	—
Rule induction	Principle components, discriminant function, factor analysis, logistic R	—
Kohonen networks	Cluster analysis, probability density function	Multidimensional cube
Spatial visualization	Two–Three dimension charts	Two–Three dimension charts
Euclidean space	Structured equations, linear and non-linear regression	Sequential files
Classification	Logistical regression	Multidimensional cube
Estimation	Regression equations, chi-square, structural equations	—
Segmentation	Cluster analysis, factor analysis	Multidimensional cube
Prediction accuracy	Statistical significance	Temporal, trend reporting
Outliers detection	Standard deviation, error analysis	Aggregation
Supervised learning	Hypothesis, distributional assumptions, APRIORI	—
Unsupervised learning	Descriptive statistics, cluster analysis	Temporal, trend reporting
Population, universe	Samples	Fact tables and dimension tables
Feature vectors	Histogram, correlation	Cross-tabs
Feature extraction	Flat files	Extract, transform, load (ETL)
Machine learning, artificial intelligence	Mathematics	Structured query language (SQL)
Attributes, features	Variables, values	Fields, records
Outputs or scoring	Independents	Fields

population can be terabytes in size, and in the very near future data mining modeling can happen to live data, called knowledge discovery in databases.

In this case, the typical steps taken by researchers to make statistical assumptions about the population are not necessary. However, understanding the database in which data reside and the data characteristics (structured and unstructured) are essential to successful data mining. Throwing all variables in a database for data mining is not conducive to machine learning. For instance, a researcher may want to identify patterns of persistence. In the dataset entered, student social security number and the corresponding college assigned student IDs and student names served no other purpose than confusing the algorithms and hogging memory. They need not be selected. However, addresses may reveal important information about a student's inclination to relocate. Sometimes the use of factor analysis or principal components to root out the auxiliary features may be desirable. The use of several techniques to cross-validate particular extrapolatives, including classical statistical techniques, is a recommended approach, called "bagging."

Data mining works best in exploratory analysis scenarios that have no preconceived assumptions (Westphal and Blaxton, 1998). *A prior* hypothesis may guide classical statistical approach but cloud the judgment of a data miner. Data mining, neural networks in particular, is most useful for prediction and scoring but not for casual statistical analysis (Garson, 1998). If the traditional methods can be viewed as top down, data mining is truly bottom up. Research questions do not begin with "what *if*," instead, they begin with "what *is*" (Luan and Willette, 2001).

As expressed earlier in the chapter, basic and classical statistical knowledge is highly useful to a data miner in discerning minute significance in cluster boundaries—an important data mining task. Neural networks are in essence regression models adapted to conduct estimation. In this sense, what was a concern to a researcher, statistical significance, is now a question of how it translates into accuracy of the prediction or classification. Data mining has set researchers free by taking the chore of making distributional assumptions about data out of their hands and giving them the power of applying machine learning models to new data. This is how data mining transforms a researcher armed with statistical skills into a data miner who drives the engine of pattern recognition and behavior prediction.

Current Trends in Data Mining

Evolving out of traditional statistics, data mining started as an independent set of tools. More and more, visualization and database data mining are adopted. Conventional visualization techniques are aimed at the executives who are information consumers. Spatial visualization provides visual plots depicting members of the population in their feature space. It is not aggregation based computation, but faithful (powerful) rendition of the geometric relationships, be it orientation, density, or clustering (Delmater and

Hancock, 2001). Also, knowledge discovery in database attempts to seamlessly integrate data mining with databases, so as to eliminate the extra work of producing additional datasets. Knowledge discovery in database maintains data consistency and, most crucially, makes real-time scoring possible. Both these trends are here to stay.

Fuzzy Logic. Another data mining algorithm being developed is fuzzy logic, which can be applied to both rule induction techniques and neural networks. Silipo (1999) argued that the opaque nature of all neural network operations would be diminished via the implementation of fuzzy logic due to its relatively transparent decisional algorithms. Berthold (1999) applied fuzzy logic to imprecise data, most commonly found in social science where crisp measurements do not exist. Even though regular neural networks have redundancy computation built in, which alleviates some of the damage done by data degradation (Silipo, 1999), the use of fuzzy logic is deemed a good alternative.

Genetic Algorithm. Genetic algorithm (GA) is an optimization algorithm developed by John Holland at the University of Michigan. It is based on the two basic rules that govern the vast organic world, selection and variation. Genetic algorithm uses selection, crossover, and mutation parameters in evolutionary computation in reaching the solution (Jacob, 1999; Berry and Linoff, 1997). Genetic algorithms fall under the class of stochastic search methods.

Applications of Data Mining

Data mining has been recently discovered by academia but was first put to full use by the Fortune 500, who have since benefited tremendously. Data mining was behind numerous successful market campaigns and quality assurance. Table 2.3 depicts some of the core questions most often used in the business world and their analogs in higher education.

Table 2.3. Comparison of Data Mining Questions in Education and the Corporate World

Questions in the Business World	Counterpart Questions in Higher Education
Who are my most profitable customers?	Who are the students taking most credit hours?
Who are my repeat website visitors?	Who are the ones likely to return for more classes?
Who are my loyal customers?	Who are the persisters at our university, college?
What clients are likely to defect to my rivals?	What type of courses can we offer to attract more students?

Data mining was first implemented for marketing outside higher education. It certainly has parallel implications and value in higher education. As discussed earlier, marketing is part of learner relationship management. Marketing concerns the service area, enrollment, annual campaign, alumni, and college image. Combined with institutional research, it expands into student feedback and satisfaction, course availability, and faculty and staff hiring. A university service area now includes on-line course offerings, thus bringing the concept of mining course data to a new dimension. Data mining is quickly becoming a mission critical component for the decision-making and knowledge management processes.

Exploring Data Mining in Higher Education: A Case Study

Using data mining to monitor and predict community college students' transfer to four-year institutions provides significant benefits for decision makers, counselors, and students. For years, institutional researchers have not been able to clearly pinpoint the type of students who transfer and their course taking patterns. Analyses of the outcomes of transferred students in upper divisions can influence the curriculum design back at the community colleges. Data mining helps predict the transferability of each currently enrolled student. A model developed in this case study is aimed at providing a profile of the transferred students and predicting which student currently enrolled in a community college will transfer so that the college can personalize and time their interactions and interventions with these students, who may need certain assistance and support. This embodies the principles of learner relationship management.

A data exchange consortium, led by the planning and research office of Cabrillo College, including Cabrillo College, University of California Santa Cruz, San Jose State University, and California State University Monterey Bay, established in 1998 a longitudinal data warehouse of transferred students, including all their course information. Taken together, the records cover 75 percent of the total annual transfers from Cabrillo College. The transfer data warehouse is then combined with the existing data warehouse of the planning and research office at Cabrillo College to provide unitary records for every student from the moment they enrolled at Cabrillo College to the day they graduated from the four-year institution. This data gold mine holds answers to many policy and research questions.

Data Mining Approach to Transfer Data. Both University of California Santa Cruz (UCSC) and San Jose State University provided data going back to 1992. California State University Monterey Bay, created in 1995, did not participate in this study because of the recency of their data. I spent a significant amount of time staging the data that came from three disparate sources. Cross industry standard process for data mining (CRISP-DM) lent guidance for this endeavor, and I have also listed steps in data preparation in the appendix of this chapter. It is a major rule in the data mining community that a data mining project cannot be successful if the investigator is not a domain expert who is very tuned to the granular data. The investigator must also have adequate skills in feature extraction, where more than 65 percent of the time can be spent on getting the features and attributes correctly presented and primed for mining purposes. The current trend is for researchers to educate themselves to master these contrasting sets of skills in order to adapt to the changing world of knowledge management.

With the outcome of transfer of students being clearly known, this was a supervised data mining. Owing to the need for predicting transfers and, as a consequence, planning for contacting these transfer-directed students, the dataset includes as much enrollment history and demographic information as possible for every student who had ever attended Cabrillo College, transferred or not. This constitutes a considerably deep and wide feature extraction. The evolution of this project is chronicled as follows.

Transfer tracking is a matter of latency. Research showed that it typically takes two to four years for the majority of the cohort to transfer. Therefore, the first task was to decide which time series in the database to use. The first year when data were available in the planning and research office data warehouse was 1992, which meant the corresponding first year of the two universities' data should be 1994. Since the last year of data that were congruent to each other from these universities was 1998, the cohort therefore should be former Cabrillo College students who enrolled between summer 1992 and spring 1997. The second task was to edit every field so that indexes could function properly. Many hidden problems, such as different coding for social security numbers and terms, were uncovered at this point, thus preventing future problems downstream. Also, data fields sent from the same university were not the same each year, when a new person was wearing the database administrator hat. The third task was to tackle the so-called "deep and wide" enrollment history data due to the nature of the original data source, governed by a transactional data structure, which meant that the enrollment data were highly normalized with enrollment records repeating for as many rows as needed for each student. Although data mining algorithms would run directly using this setup, it could only produce completely erroneous conclusions. Each subsequent enrollment record of a student needed to become a field by itself, a requirement that brought on the issue of dealing with potentially many dozens of fields for just the courses taken without yet introducing the grades for the courses and the term in which the student took each of the courses. The final dataset was a result of collapsing courses based on their type (transfer, remedial, vocational) at the expense of term and individual grades.

The total number of students in the dataset was thirty-two thousand. A proprietary data split algorithm divided the set into a test set and a validation set. Data mining was applied to the test set, until such time when the models were considered optimal. The validation set, first time seen by all the models, was brought in for actual scoring.

The following is a partial list of the groups of features (fields) selected for this case study:

- Demographics: age, gender, ethnicity, high school, zip codes, planned employment hours, education status at initial enrollment
- Financial aid
- Transfer status (doubled as the reference variable)
- Total transfer, vocational, basic skills, science, and liberal arts courses taken
- Total units earned and grade points by course type

Clementine, a software by SPSS Inc., enjoys a reputation for being the easiest model to deploy. The study chose Clementine as the data mining software (please refer to Chapter Six for data mining tools). Experience led me to use neural networks (NN) and two rule induction algorithms, C5.0 and C&RT, to compare models and to complement the scoring. As already mentioned, some data mining experts call this "bagging." The type node in Clementine coded the fields into appropriate types, and the balance node reduced the imbalance between transferred and nontransferred students, which was quite large initially.

The NN model resulted in an accuracy of 76.5 percent. It contained fifty-two neurons, seven hidden neurons, and one neuron (for a dichotomous output). The top ten fields listed in the relative importance of inputs were

Number of liberal arts classes taken (0.315)
High school origin (0.189)
Race (0.161)
Planned work hours (0.159)
Initial education status (0.145)
Grade points (0.085)
Number of nonbasic skills courses taken (0.084)
Number of UCSC transferable courses taken (0.081)
Gender (0.079)
Number of degree applicable courses taken (0.074)

The values in parenthesis would range from zero to one, but in practice they were rarely above the 0.35 threshold. A couple of points worth noting here are that the investigator should pay attention to every field, even the one listed at the bottom, as data mining is both a task to identify the averages and rule of thumbs and a task to use outliers for a number of reasons, such as fraud detection. As neural networks results were a bit cryptic, it was necessary to use a rule induction model to list the rules uncovered. The following resulted from C5.0:

Rules for Transferred
Rule #1 for Transferred:
if units > 12
and # of nontransfer course ≤ 5
and # of math > 0
then transferred → (452, 0.877)

Rule #2 for Transferred:
if gender = F
and # of nontransfer course ≤ 5
and # of math > 0
then → transferred (278, 0.871)

Rule #3 for Transferred:
if age >19.9
and age ≤ 24
and grade points ≥ 5
and # of UCSC transferable courses > 0
and # of precollegiate basic skills course ≤ 0
and # of vocational course ≤ 5
and # of math ≤ 0
then → transferred (29, 0.806)

Rules for Not Transferred:
Rule #1 for Not Transferred:
if race = Hispanic
and # of SJSU transferable course ≤ 21
and # of nontransferable course > 6
and # of math ≤ 3
then → not transferred (24, 0.962)

Rule #2 for Not Transferred:
if # of UCSC transferable course ≤ 7
then → not transferred (403, 0.736)

The first value in the parenthesis was the number of cases supporting this rule and the second value the confidence. The case study then used the C&RT node to generate a decision tree with the following tree branches:

Units < 21.5 [mode: not transferred] (369)
Units < 5.5 (156, 0.955) → not transferred
Units ≥ 5.5 [mode: not transferred] (213)
NTRCRS < 2.5 [mode: not transferred] (165)
Nontransferable courses ≥ 2.5 (48, 0.938) → not transferred
UNITS ≥ 21.5 [mode: transferred] (974)

MATH ≤ 0.5 [mode: transferred] (197)
UCCRS < 13.5 (83, 0.554) → not transferred
UCSC transferable courses ≥ 13.5 (114, 0.754) → transferred
Math ≥ 0.5 (777, 0.874) → transferred

Model Analysis. Clementine provides an efficient way to compare the classification for the test set and the scoring for the validation set. Table 2.4 contains the matrixes detailing these findings.

As indicated by these matrixes, the neural networks model produced decent and somewhat balanced accuracy but not as good when compared to the C&RT model. C5.0 provided the highest accuracy for predicting students who had transferred, but it was far less accurate in predicting nontransferred. Overall, C&RT appeared to be the best model to use.

C5.0 initially produced a perfect estimation with close to 100 percent accuracy. This was a signal of the model memorizing the rules, not necessarily learning the rules. Adjustment in the number of records allowed for each split and quickly eliminated this problem. During this process, the dataset had to be rebuilt twice due to informational redundancy (correlation) concerns.

Data mining is an iterative process and identifying patterns is even more so. It is highly possible that with enough time devoted to preparing the data and adjusting the model, a higher accuracy rate (<90 percent) is possible. Ideally, the research department will be able to overlay data mining on college data warehouse and use the above model to score new students on a yearly basis. This is a true end-to-end data mining solution. The counseling department can use the list containing students scored to be "transferring inclined" for targeted mailing and personalized assistance.

Table 2.4. Matrixes of Model Performance for Test and Validation Sets

Neural Networks on Test Set	NoTran	Tran	On Validation Set	NoTran	Tran
NoTran	67.9	32.1	NoTran	78.7	21.3
Tran	20.8	79.2	Tran	22.5	77.5

C5.0 on Test Set	NoTran	Tran	On Validation Set	NoTran	Tran
NoTran	72.1	28.0	NoTran	70.0	30.0
Tran	12.5	87.5	Tran	8.0	92.0

C&RT on Test Set	NoTran	Tran	On Validation Set	Notran	Tran
NoTran	81.3	18.7	NoTran	82.8	17.2
Tran	18.4	81.6	Tran	17.9	82.1

There are three additional strategies researchers may use when conducting data mining. The first is verifying the results by classical statistics for which Clementine has provided nodes such as linear regression and logistic regression. Applying the logistic regression node to the test set resulted in an identified group of most significant features, but they are ordered differently either due to their level of significance or the internal functions of the model. Nonetheless, it covered the spectrum very well. The second strategy is to use factor analysis and principle component analysis to weed out nonsignificant variables or variables that are highly correlated with each other. However, it is worthwhile to point out that data mining is very tolerant of correlated variables, compared to the classical statistics with which we are familiar. The third strategy is one that I highly recommend. The researcher should consider clustering and segmentation analysis using TwoStep, K-means, or Kohonen even though the target field(s) is known. For example, K-means can reveal that students sharing similar characteristics may form five or six giant clusters in the data. This gives the researcher additional insights into the population and may prompt the researcher to divide the population into cluster datasets with which the data mining algorithm can significantly increase its accuracy. I applied this strategy when mining for persistence and found that by concentrating on the students who were clustered by their educational goals and the type of courses taken, the model produced far better results.

Conclusion

Synthesizing the vast amount of research and ideas and condensing them into one chapter with the aim of introducing data mining to the institutional research audience in higher education is great challenge. By using well-defined algorithms from the disciplines of machine learning and artificial intelligence to discern rules, associations, and likelihood of events, data mining has profound application significance. If it were not for the fast, vast, and real-time pattern identification and event prediction for enhanced business purposes, there would not have been such an exponential growth in dissertations, models, and the considerable amount of investment in data mining in the corporate world.

As we have discovered, insights from data sets and variable lists, previously seen as unwieldy and chaotic, can be obtained with data mining and developed into the foundations for program planning or to resolve operational issues. The power of data mining lies in the fact that it simultaneously enhances output and reduces cost. The One-Percent doctrine (Luan, 2000) states that a 1 percent change means one unit of gain and one unit in savings. For example, a 1 percent increase in enrollment may mean $500,000 for a typical college of twenty thousand students, and it is achieved with no additional cost. Data mining conducted for alumni donations may correctly pinpoint the right donors and the right target amount. This saves campaign costs and increases the campaign's effectiveness. The ability to provide intervention to individual students who are seen as likely to drop out or to transfer also holds value beyond cost and savings. Data mining conducted to predict the likelihood of an applicant's enrollment following their initial application may allow the college to send the right kind of materials to potential students and prepare the right counseling for them. The potential of data mining in education cannot be underestimated.

Appendix: Steps for Data Mining Preparation, Based on Cross Industry Standard Process for Data Mining (CRISP-DM)

- *Step One.* Investigate the possibility of overlaying data mining algorithms directly on a data warehouse. Doing so may require extra effort and diplomatic skills with the information technology department, but it pays off in the long run. It avoids possible errors in field names, unexpected changes in data types, and extra effort to refresh multiple data domains. The scoring can also be directly performed to live database. This is called an end-to-end data mining solution, also called knowledge discovery in database (KDD). (Total time usage: 5 to 15 percent.)
- *Step Two.* Select a solid querying tool to build data mining files. These files closely resemble multidimensional cubes. As a matter of fact, MOLAP (multidimensional on-line analytical processing) serves this purpose well. Except for APRIORI, which can use transactional data files directly (alas!), all other algorithms need "tabular" files, which are relational database files queried to produce a file with unique records with multiple fields. A number of querying tools are available for this purpose. SQL skills are highly desirable. This step can be most time consuming. (Total time usage: 30 to 75 percent.)
- *Step Three.* Data visualization and validation. This means examining frequency counts as well as generating scatter plots, histograms, and other graphics, including clustering models. A graph is the best indication for a correlation estimate. This step gives the researcher the first impression of what each of the data fields contains and how it may play out in the analysis. Missing data should not be treated in the same manner in every situation. In certain cases, missing data are extremely diagnostic. In data mining, the outliers may be just what we are looking for, simply because they deviate from the norm. Therefore, they may hold truth for discovering previously unknown patterns. In fraud detection, it is these outliers that will flag the system to avoid loss. (Total time usage: 10 to 20 percent.)
- *Step Four.* Mine your data! (Total time usage: 10 to 20 percent.)

References

Berry, M., and Linoff, G. *Data Mining Technique: For Marketing, Sales, and Customer Support*. New York: Wiley Computer Publishing, 1997.

Berry, M., and Linoff, G. *Master Data Mining: The Art and Science of Customer Relationship Management*. New York: Wiley Computer Publishing, 2000.

Berthold, M. "Fuzzy Logic." In M. Berthold and D. Hand (eds.), *Intelligent Data Analysis*. Milan: Springer, 1999.

Brieman, L. "Comment." *Statistical Science*, 1994, 9(1), 38–42.

Delmater, R., and Hancock, M. *Data Mining Explained: A Manager's Guide to Customer-Centric Business Intelligence*. Boston: Digital Press, 2001.

De Veaux, R. "Data Mining: What's New, What's Not." Presentation at a Data Mining Workshop, Long Beach, Calif., 2000.

Garson, G. D. *Neural Networks: An Introductory Guide for Social Scientists*. London: Sage, 1998.

Gartner Group. "The GartnerGroup CRM Glossary." [http://www.gartnerweb.com/public/static/hotc/hc00086148.html].

Hand, D. "Introduction." In M. Berthold and D. Hand (eds.), *Intelligent Data Analysis*. Milan: Springer, 1999.

Jacob, C. "Stochastic Search Method." In M. Berthold and D. Hand (eds.), *Intelligent Data Analysis*. Milan: Springer, 1999.

Luan, J. "An Exploratory Approach to Data Mining in Higher Education: A Primer and a Case Study." Paper presented at the AIR Forum, Seattle, Wash., 2000.

Luan, J., and Willette, T. "Data Mining and Knowledge Management." Paper presented at the Research and Planning Group Conference, Lake Arrowhead, Calif., 2001.

Mena, J. "Data-Mining FAQs." *DM Review*, January 1998. [http://www.dmreview.com/master.cfm?NAVID=198&EdiD=792].

Roueche, J. E., and Roueche, S. S. *High Stakes, High Performance: Making Remediation Work*. Washington, D.C.: Community College Press, 1999.

Rubenking, N. "Hidden Messages." *PC Magazine*, May 22, 2001, 20(10), 86–88.

Silipo, R. "Neural Networks." In M. Berthold and D. Hand (eds.), *Intelligent Data Analysis*. Milan: Springer, 1999.

SPSS. *SPSS Clementine 6.0 User's Guide*. Chicago: SPSS, 2001.

Statsoft. [http://www.statsoft.com/textbook/glosfra.html], 2001.

Thearling, K. "An Overview of Data Mining at Dun and Bradstreet." *DIG White Paper*, 1995. [http://www3.shore.net/~kht/text/wp9501/wp9501.html].

van den Eijkel, G. C. "Rule Induction." In M. Berthold and D. Hand (eds.), *Intelligent Data Analysis*. Milan: Springer, 1999.

Watkins, D. "Neural Network Master Class." Presented at Clementine User Group (CLUG), July 2000, Reading, United Kingdom.

Westphal, C., and Blaxton, T. *Data Mining Solutions: Methods and Tools for Solving Real-World Problems*. New York: Wiley Computer Publishing, 1998.

JING LUAN is chief planning and research officer at Cabrillo College in Aptos, California.

3

Portals are the first "killer" applications of knowledge management due to their versatility, broad technical and functional capabilities, and ease of use. Well-designed portals allow institutions to create and implement the knowledge management strategy of their choice. This chapter presents the elements, components, and processes involved in setting and maintaining portals. It uses Santa Barbara City College as a case study of a portal implementation with the purpose of supporting knowledge management, and it underscores the role played and benefits gained by institutional research and the college as a result.

Building Portals for Higher Education

Richard A. Pickett, William B. Hamre

This chapter explores the underlying purposes and architecture for the use of portal technology as the keystone for knowledge management systems in higher education. The discussion of portal technology is exemplified by Santa Barbara City College's development of portal strategies and processes to support the college's Intranet.

There are many definitions of a portal. Gartner Group includes four basic components in its definition of a portal: connection, content, commerce, and community (Yanosky, 2000). Santa Barbara City College has developed the following working definition for its knowledge management project: "A portal is a personalized collection of information, content, and services." Personalization is a key to a successful knowledge management implementation, as it provides access to targeted information based on individual roles and responsibilities within the institution. The collection of disparate content into a well-structured personal portal page is also an important element of success in the design and implementation of a portal. Finally, the portal must provide more than simple access to data. It must provide the search, navigation, analytical, and communication tools necessary for members of the institution's community to do their work in a collaborative manner.

Santa Barbara City College's Project Redesign and Portal Development

For the past six years, Santa Barbara City College has undertaken a systematic and wide-ranging assessment of institutional effectiveness and reengineering of college business practices in its Project Redesign initiative (Rudy, 1996). The college has approached the development of its college Intranet from the perspective of implementing many of the recommendations of the

NEW DIRECTIONS FOR INSTITUTIONAL RESEARCH, no. 113, Spring 2002 © Wiley Periodicals, Inc.

redesign teams. Recent developments in portal technologies and tools have allowed the institution to design and develop Intranet applications to meet the objectives of Project Redesign and provide a framework for knowledge management within the institution.

The institution's key goals for its Intranet portal include the following:

- Improve access to college information
- Improve understanding and use of college information
- Improve institutional decision making
- Improve collaboration and communication among college departments

The college has identified a number of key components that must be in place within its knowledge management framework for the institution to achieve these goals. Of primary importance is the development of a decision support system to support and enhance the operational, evaluation, research, and planning functions within the institution. A second key area is document management. All college policies, procedures, reports, meeting agendas and minutes, and key college publications will be included within the knowledge management portal. Electronic forms and workflow capabilities are essential to support the improvement and automation of Santa Barbara City College business processes. More effective mechanisms for Web content development and administration are also important components of the knowledge management project. Expanded use of college e-mail alerts and notifications, as well as structures for increasing college communications, are objectives of the project. Finally, database security and management provide the technical infrastructure to implement a robust and secure knowledge management system.

The college Intranet portal project is a joint initiative of the information resources division and the office of institutional assessment, research, and planning. The development of decision support information is at the heart of this project. As such, the role of the office of institutional assessment, research, and planning is critical to the success of the portal project. The college cabinet and college planning council provide overall project leadership and direction. Key decisions must be made regarding information architecture, analytical tools, and access security. The information systems development team and the office of institutional assessment, research, and planning should make these decisions jointly. Lack of cooperation, planning, and skills development between these entities will place such projects at risk. Institutional researchers must become core members of the institution's Web development team during the design, development, and deployment of a campus Intranet portal.

What Is a Portal?

As we all know the Internet has become an integrated component of our work and personal lives. The number of Web hosts has grown from 1.3 million in 1993 to over a hundred million at the beginning of 2001 (Internet

Software Consortium, *Internet Domain Survey,* 2001). These hosts generate approximately one billion URLs (Universal Resource Locators). Gartner Group estimates that by 2003 more than 90 percent of government entities will deploy one or more portals to serve their constituencies (Di Maio, 2001). As discussed in Chapter One, we are being inundated with a growing amount of information, a situation that creates a strong need to find a method of organizing the information that is pertinent for our interests and responsibilities. Portals provide such organization. Ryland (2000) points out the importance of effective knowledge navigation, and "finds us at the very early stages of understanding how to manage and navigate through the huge volumes of information and knowledge being made available through the World Wide Web on the Internet."

Web portals are one of the most popular topics of discussion in technology today. With so much written on portals one would assume that a common definition would be available. Frequently we find that these definitions do not synchronize with each other. Some people see this as a problem; we see this as an opportunity. In fact, that is the beauty of a portal, each person can have his or her own definition. A definition of a basic portal is rather simple: a gateway to network-accessible resources (Intranet, Extranet, and Internet). A simple Web page could fit this definition, as could a complex site composed of thousands of Web pages. Some of the early portals were quite simple, offering their visitors a static view of content from a small number of sources.

As our user communities have become aware of the Internet, their expectation of a usable and acceptable Web portal has risen. No longer are people satisfied to use a generic portal that is designed to meet the lowest common denominator of all of the target audiences. Today there is an increased need for personal portals. A personal portal is one that is personalized and potentially customizable for a particular individual. These portals should be dynamic, providing each individual user with their own view of the information resources that is current.

Commercial examples of portals include my.oracle.com, my.yahoo.com, excite.com, and many others. Individual organizations are increasingly building their own corporate portals for both Internet and Intranet use. This chapter provides information on how colleges and universities can build and benefit from these portals and more specifically how they can assist institutional research efforts.

Why Are Portals Useful?

There is one major reason for portals, efficiency. Portals help make more efficient use of an individual's time, one of the most important organizational resources. With the ever-increasing glut of data, it is essential to provide an organization's constituencies with focused information that can facilitate better decision making. Moore (2001) points out the importance of integration of applications, rather than a simple collection of content, within the portal. A portal will never provide a person with all of their informational needs. An organization can create a gateway, however, that should provide a significant amount of core information. Again, personalization of portal content is an important element in making the campus Intranet useful to a broad set of constituents. Borck (2001) points out the emerging importance of "context personalization" for personalized portal applications, based on factors such as a user's current task, time of day, accessing device, bandwidth, and location.

Importance to Institutional Research

A great deal of organizational information is stored, in various forms, in the data that are collected through the daily operations of a college or university. In some cases it is important to provide immediate access to the data in order to make short-term decisions, in other cases information is aggregated, verified, and summarized to provide a longer-term perspective. One of the challenges for offices of institutional research is the development of methods to deliver this information to those individuals and offices that can benefit most. Frequently this information is filed away or published in formats that are not conducive to frequent, broad, and immediate dissemination. A Web portal can increase the distribution of this information dramatically and can do so in a secure manner.

Using a personalized and focused design, information that previously was difficult to access can be published in a Business Intelligence Portal (BIP). Frequently, Web sites are designed to provide only a static view of information; an effective institutional portal can integrate dynamic query and display of data, thereby greatly increasing the utilization of critical knowledge for institutional decision making.

Portal Architecture

A Web site, or portal, consists of several hardware and software components that perform the functions of servicing the user's requests and assembling the necessary information for delivery through a Web browser. Many of these components share the term *server*, whether they consist of computer software or hardware. The software components can reside either on separate hardware servers or be colocated on a single device. The hardware architecture decision is usually determined based upon the projected demands on the Web site. A well-designed Web site should be able to accommodate growth and provide for flexibility in hardware configuration as the needs of the organization change. Typically a Web site consists of the following software components:

- Web server
- File system or database
- Application server

Figure 3.1. Portal Architecture

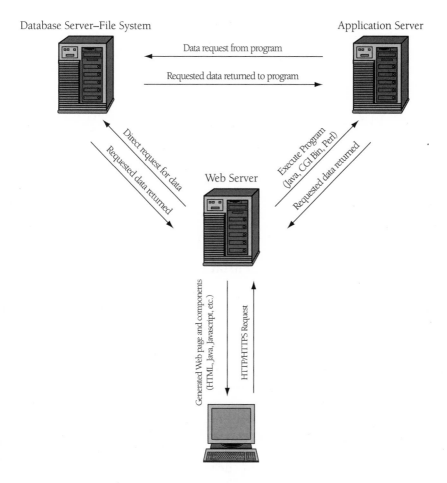

Figure 3.1 provides a high-level overview of the portal architecture.

The Web server provides the initial connection link between the user's Web browser (Netscape Communicator, Microsoft Internet Explorer) and the Web pages using the Hypertext Transfer Protocol (HTTP) or the secure version of HTTP—HTTPS. When the Web server receives the request for a page, it determines the appropriate service to provide that information. If the requested page contains static information, such as text or graphics, the information may simply be retrieved from the server's file system. In many cases, the information will reside in multiple locations, requiring the Web server to send additional requests to the remote content providers. After the information is collected, the Web server will send the completed information back to the requesting user.

Frequently Web pages contain additional functionality such as searching, calculations, and other actions. The application server (which can be an integral component of the Web server) provides these functions with the capability to execute these requests. The applications could be designed in Java, C, Perl, or a variety of other languages. The application server also can manage the authentication and authorization functions for those sites that require secure access.

Web sites increasingly store only a limited portion of their information as static pages. The majority of portal Web pages are dynamic—the pages do not exist until a user requests them. These dynamic pages are composed of various components that may exist at different locations, both internal and external to an organization. The components are assembled based upon the specific request and then delivered via the Web server to the users.

In conjunction with a single user sign-on and interface, this architecture allows the personalization of content through the collection and presentation of multiple portal components: applications, services, tools, and data.

Santa Barbara City College Portal Functionality and Framework

The institution must have a well-defined portal architecture and toolset before successful planning and implementation can begin. Santa Barbara City College has identified four major components of our portal strategy: decision support and data warehousing, document management, Web site management, and content communications. Figure 3.2 provides an overview of Santa Barbara City College's portal components and architecture.

This section describes these components in detail and discusses the specific technologies that Santa Barbara City College is using to implement portal technology in relation to its knowledge management initiative. Key software tools within Santa Barbara City College's portal implementation include WebCT for courseware development and delivery, Campus Pipeline for student Web access, iPlanet for messaging and calendar services, Oracle Portal for Intranet development, and Oracle Database and Applications for electronic forms and workflow. The selection of specific vendor tools must be undertaken with an eye toward the integration of multiple tools into an overall campus architecture. For Santa Barbara City College, the recent integration of WebCT and Campus Pipeline into a single sign-on, session management, and course framework was a significant step forward in providing a user-friendly and intuitive framework for our students. In building their campus portals, institutions have used different vendors and tools successfully. Chapter Six provides additional information regarding some of the available options. Santa Barbara City College's selection of portal toolsets has been conditioned largely by the selection by faculty of the WebCT product for instructional courseware development and delivery and on the selection of Oracle Applications for campus administrative systems.

Figure 3.2. Santa Barbara City College Portal Framework

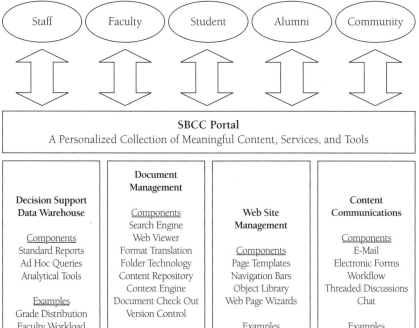

Decision Support

A key goal of any knowledge management implementation must be to structure information to assist in college decision making. While "executive information systems" have been components of many campus administrative information systems, the advent of portal technology offers several new capabilities. By far the most important of these is the ability to personalize the content of the decision support system based on user responsibilities and individual preferences.

At Santa Barbara City College, the initial focus of decision support activities has been to support academic program review, college planning and resource rankings, institutional effectiveness assessment, and accreditation. Roueche, Ely, and Roueche (2001) point out the importance of such institutional assessment in describing the Community College of Denver's pursuit of excellence. Common measures of institutional effectiveness are used for many of these purposes. Measures of successful course completions, faculty load, and productivity are used on an institutional basis in its annual assessment of institutional effectiveness. The academic senate and college planning council use these same measures at the departmental level to make decisions concerning the ranking of new faculty positions. Division deans and department chairs use these same measures during the evaluation of individual faculty members.

Effective use of information to support these multiple purposes requires several capabilities. Access to data must be controlled by the role or responsibilities of individuals within the organization. Specifically, institutional policy decisions concerning access to departmental and individual faculty data must be supported by the database application. In addition, it must be easy for users to navigate through the various levels of organizational hierarchies through "drill down" and "roll up" capabilities. Flexibility also must be provided in the availability of analytical tools to support the personalization of the decision support system, as individuals use and analyze data in many different ways.

The decision support function of the institutional knowledge management system is a primary responsibility of the office of institutional assessment, research, and planning at Santa Barbara City College. This responsibility includes guiding the institutional discussions of appropriate measures to be used, designing data warehouse structures, developing standard reports and query templates, as well as training college faculty and management to use the tools and information effectively in support of their respective roles. It was a very deliberate decision by the college to place these functions within this office. There were several reasons for this decision. First, the college needed a central department to coordinate the design and development of the institution's decision support systems. The institutional research function has a collegewide perspective of information structures, reporting, and use. Second, the institutional research function has the technical expertise to use data management and analytical tools effectively. Finally, and perhaps most important, the office is charged with defining the implications for college practice from all research studies and data analyses conducted on campus. Research and analysis are of very limited use to the institution unless they are constantly applied to determine how the institution can improve the quality and responsiveness of its operations and services.

At Santa Barbara City College, this pivotal role is assigned to the office of institutional assessment, research, and planning. This responsibility places very broad demands on this office: database design, data analysis, policy development, and technology planning and implementation. Some offices of institutional research may be reluctant to undertake these broadened areas of responsibilities. This expanded role for the institutional research function is, however, a natural outcome of increased institutional focus on data driven decision making and accountability. These added responsibilities also place additional demands on the ability of the institutional research office to recruit, train, and retain staff conversant in research methodologies, analytical tools, Web development, databases, and higher education policy.

Document Management

College policies, procedures, and operational processes must be stored and retrieved easily. This requirement poses many organizational and technical challenges for the designers of institutional knowledge management systems. Support for document management is an essential component of knowledge management.

The use of structured, hierarchical document storage taxonomies versus "unstructured" search capabilities is a key design decision for institutions. Santa Barbara City College chose to emphasize the latter approach due to reduced maintenance costs and increased flexibility for information access. For this approach to be successful, however, the search engine must be able to conduct full-text searches of archived documents, rather than relying on key words, abstracts, or titles. While these capabilities are now part of all desktop operating systems, the extension to all campus policies, procedures, and official documents requires a very robust and efficient search mechanism to deal with the hundreds of institutional documents contained on the college Intranet (or in the college Intranet environment).

Establishing standards for document storage and viewing formats also presents challenges for institutions. Santa Barbara City College made the decision to provide browser-based access to all documents contained in the knowledge management database or "repository." Early on, this meant conversion of documents to HTML and centralized posting of documents by our Web development department. With the implementation of the Oracle Portal product technology, the process for storage and retrieval of documents has been much improved. Files are stored in the database in their native formats (Word, Excel, PDF [portable document format], HTML [hypertext mark-up language], and so forth) but are viewed through a Web browser without required plug-ins due to "on the fly" translation of these file formats to HTML. This capability saves much time in file creation and maintenance within the college Intranet system. These stored documents also can be accessed directly by users from the database in their native formats.

Understanding the context of key word search results is another design component of document management. This component includes having an efficient weighting system for prioritizing search results. Along with the weighting algorithm, the Oracle Portal, using the integrated Oracle Text capability, develops *themes* and *gists* for each document stored in the document management repository. The thematic analysis is based upon an extensible thesaurus. The listing of themes outlines the central concepts presented in each document so that one can navigate quickly to the desired area. Gists present summary statements in narrative form of the key themes within each document. These capabilities assist users in understanding the context and content of documents contained within the knowledge management database, and are made possible through the use of a linguistics engine that is part of the Oracle Portal environment. Document versioning, end-dating, archiving, access control, and security are also important elements of document management capabilities that are a product of using a database for storage of documents within a knowledge management system.

These document management capabilities allow for rapid and efficient navigation of the institution's policies, procedures, and publications. A student or faculty member with questions concerning campus policies on grading can simply enter "grading" into the search engine and rapidly retrieve all Intranet documents containing the term. The individual can then navigate quickly internally within the documents to find specific highlighted references to grading. Themes from these documents, such as academic probation or grade point average, are also referenced to provide users with more refined choices for viewing. Campus directory information is another good example of the deployment to this technology. An on-line directory provides up-to-the-minute listings of college personnel and directory information that can be accessed easily by first name, last name, building, department, or other directory attributes.

Prior to the development of the college Intranet, these document management features were nonexistent at Santa Barbara City College. The function of storage and retention of documents was highly decentralized, with many differing departmental policies, tools, and practices. College standardization of these elements within the Intranet project has led to a far more comprehensive, useful, and powerful repository of campus electronic documents. This framework is an ideal way for offices of institutional research to make their publications available to their campus community. Adding research reports and publications to the document repository is easy to do. Once in the repository, for example, a study on the effectiveness of on-line instruction will be returned in the search results on queries for grading, retention, technology, and many other terms. This leads to greater dissemination and use of institutional research reports.

Web Content Development and Management

Web site content creation and management present a specialized case of document management functionality. Decentralization of Web content development and posting was a key objective for Santa Barbara City College's knowledge management Intranet application. The college had experienced great difficulty in training and support in HTML and FTP (file transfer protocol) for departmental Web developers. In addition, the enforcement of design and navigation standards within departmental development proved problematic. These problems required that all Web content be routed to the Web development group to provide quality assurance and final posting to the college Web site. This process simply was not sustainable for the development and maintenance of the college's knowledge management Web site. The Oracle Portal technology provides end-user tools for the construction and maintenance of Web pages through a Web browser interface. Since these elements are stored directly into the portal database, there is no need for separate file transfer processes. The use of any such tool necessarily constrains page structure and functionality to some extent. For Santa Barbara City College, however, the significant gains in departmental Web development productivity have been well worth such constraints.

Dynamic Web page deployment is a key to the personalization of knowledge management systems. This requires that the individual's view of a Web page be built "on the fly" according to specific user roles, preferences, and access to information. Harris and Caldwell (2000) point out the need for "compelling technology" to support effective knowledge management systems. This move away from static, uniform HTML pages places significantly increased reliance and importance on the database capabilities of the institution. Individual user responsibilities, security, and preferences must be maintained in data structures that can support the rapid collection, assembly, and deployment of individual Web pages. This component-based approach to Web site construction allows for the re-use of templates, graphics, documents, and applications throughout the Web site.

Decentralization of Santa Barbara City College Web site content development and management is a major objective for our Intranet portal project. Our previous model for Web site maintenance had departmental Web page developers preparing content and then transferring that content to a holding area for review and posting by the college's Web development team (consisting of one Web master and one Web developer). This centralized approach provided quality assurance and standards review of pages before posting, but at great cost in terms of productivity of our Web development staff. In the new model, departmental content developers are given the ability to construct pages based on approved templates and using a central library of Web objects. Review of a Web page before posting has shifted from the Web development group to the departmental manager, who focuses on the accuracy and completeness of the page content. This direction is intended to provide more time for limited Web development resources to work on more technical issues, such as systems integration and security.

These Web content capabilities allow the office of institutional assessment, research, and planning to design, develop, and maintain a Web-based content area for research studies, reports, ad hoc queries, and analytical tools. The look and feel of the institutional research site can be customized within the institution's standard departmental page templates and tools. The use of development "wizards" allows institutional researchers to develop Web-based delivery without requiring them to become experts in HTML, XML, or Java. This self-sufficiency for the offices of institutional research is a real benefit to those departments constantly trying to battle for information resource support with other college operating units. Again, the institutional research office must be viewed as an integral part of the college's Web development team if campus objectives on improved decision making are to be realized.

Content Communications

Knowledge Management systems present opportunities for the automation of college forms and workflow to restructure institutional business processes. While most institutions have deployed Web technology to present electronic forms to the college community, far fewer have undertaken a systematic and rigorous management of their business processes with automated workflow engines. There are several reasons for this relatively slow adoption of workflow technology. First, institutions must invest the time and resources to document existing business processes in a consistent structure and methodology. This is a time-consuming and labor-intensive process. Santa Barbara City College spent three years using more than thirty project teams to document key business processes targeted for redesign through business process reengineering. The college experienced great difficulty in freeing key staff members to participate in these redesign sessions. A second roadblock to workflow automation has been the relative immaturity of the technology itself. Workflow tools have begun to deepen in product capabilities and simplify in terms of ease of use. Investment in workflow technology at the current time, however, means training of technology staff in the sometimes arcane use of workflow tools. The industry is still a long way away from providing simple end-user tools for automating and managing college workflow processes. A final reason for the slow adoption of workflow technology is the continuing maintenance and support needed to keep these systems current with changes in institutional process over time. Once the systems have been developed via workflow technology, revisions to college processes must be re-implemented by using the workflow engine.

Given these limitations, why would higher education institutions adopt processing strategies of electronic forms and automated workflow? The reasons are many. Most important, these technologies allow for the potential for saving much time and effort in the conduct of institutional business processes. Forms implemented in knowledge management systems can be routed simultaneously to multiple individuals for review and approval. In addition, college business rules for edit checks and calculations and institutional rules for routing and approval of documents can be enforced systematically without relying on the knowledge of the initiator on how to process the document. Capturing and storing process workflows and business rules also insulate the institution from the loss of key personnel who maintain the knowledge of proper procedures in their heads. As discussed in Chapter One, far too often we bemoan the loss of key college staff and the institutional knowledge and history they take with them. The discipline and rigor associated with mapping institutional business processes and workflows also provide a wonderful opportunity for reexamining current business practices and procedures.

The implementation of portal technology is key to the successful implementation of a streamlined workflow process. Hayward (2000) notes the importance of conceiving of knowledge management as "not the implementation of a technology; rather, it is a multidiscipline approach that integrates business strategy, cultural values, and work processes." The individual's portal page becomes the central point of collection of tasks and activities from many different systems. A faculty member, for example, can receive class lists and rosters, initiate student drops, submit grades, initiate requisitions, conduct campus library searches, and analyze departmental performance data all from the same portal framework. Although the systems integration work of a portal implementation is a major undertaking, the rewards are substantial for end users in terms of ease of use.

Collaboration tools such as e-mail, discussion groups, chat, Web conferencing, workflow, alerts, and document sharing are essential components of the portal framework. These tools provide synchronous and asynchronous methods of communication and resource sharing among individuals and various constituencies of the college community. Integration of these various tools within the portal framework can be very challenging from a technical perspective, but is essential to realizing the time and resource saving potential of the institutional portal.

Identification of Communities

A first step in the definition of a campus portal is the identification of communities of interest to be served by the portal. What are the groups on campus that need to communicate and to have access to similar kinds of information? Once these communities are defined, the institution can begin planning the specific set of documents, information, forms, and services to be made available to each group. At Santa Barbara City College we have used the college Web committee to define these communities of interest, and then have used the college cabinet for the review and approval of these portal communities and services.

Toolset Evaluation

As discussed in Chapter Six, there are many portal providers and toolsets available to institutions of higher education, and many different approaches can be taken. Individual decisions by institutions are conditioned by many factors, including the following: current technology environment, technical expertise available at the institution, level of staffing for development and support, and project funding to name a few. At Santa Barbara City College, for example, our choice of Campus Pipeline as a student portal framework was influenced significantly by its partnership with WebCT to integrate the instructional content development and delivery mechanisms of WebCT into the portal framework of Campus Pipeline under a single sign-on and authentication process. As we had committed previously to WebCT as our institutional toolset for instructional content management, portal vendor integration with WebCT loomed large in our decision process. Likewise, our selection of Oracle's Portal product for college Intranet development was influenced by our preexisting campus licensing agreement for Oracle database and applications development products (Portal is an integral component of Oracle's Internet Application Server product) and our use of Oracle applications for the college's administrative systems.

Regardless of the unique institutional circumstances, there are some important considerations that are common across institutions in terms of portal toolset selection. The Gartner Group has identified five criteria for institutional evaluation of portal framework products: robust search across all structured and unstructured repositories, taxonomy support, content management and aggregation, personalization, and application integration and development (Phifer and Zastrocky, 2000).

Data Warehouse Design

The development of an effective decision support system for the college is a primary objective of Santa Barbara City College's portal project. Previous institutional efforts in this area have not been successful due to several factors. First, development and maintenance resources have been limited to grant funding and were not sustainable by ongoing staff due to other systems development and maintenance tasks. Second, the use and navigation of client-based analytical tools were viewed as too cumbersome by campus managers. Third, and perhaps most important, managers lacked the time necessary to do detailed analysis of data provided in the data warehouse. These "lessons learned" by Santa Barbara City College in previous projects helped provide design objectives for the decision support functionality within the campus Intranet portal project.

Key measures need to be identified for each person or role using the portal. These measures will facilitate the personalization of the portal. The elements and level of detail that are needed by the president are significantly different from those of the vice presidents, deans, and department chairs. We need to create a customized "executive dashboard" for each of these roles within the institution. This dashboard needs to reflect information that is current and relevant to the decisions being made in each role. During registration, for example, department chairs and deans are monitoring course enrollments in order to make decisions on adding or canceling course sections. Both of these roles need to be able to view enrollment data—department chairs for their specific department and deans for all departments within their area. Easy access to this structured set of data is important for timely and effective decision making during registration. While many other individuals within the institution are interested in such course enrollment data and should be able to query such information, it would not appear on their dashboard for action. Individual faculty members, for example, may want to save a query of course enrollments in their classes as an object on their portal page. Such personalized extension of the portal page is an important element of the success and usefulness of the portal application.

As noted previously, the focus of Santa Barbara City College's data warehousing strategy is to support institutional assessment, planning, resource allocation, and departmental program review activities. By design, there are many common measures that are used across these areas. Student course completion rates, grade distributions, faculty workload and productivity, full-time equivalent students, and full-time to part-time faculty ratios are examples of measures that serve many planning and evaluation purposes. Careful attention must be paid to the levels of aggregation, related variables, and security of these data in the data warehouse design. At Santa Barbara City College, the director of institutional assessment, research, and planning has the responsibility for the design and development of the data warehouse model, with assistance as needed from the information resources division in terms of data development and transformation. The college cabinet members work directly with the office of institutional assessment, research, and planning in defining the key measures of effectiveness to be used in their areas of responsibility.

Security Design

Access to specific pages, content, data elements, and levels of detail ideally is controlled by security measures within the portal database of users, responsibilities, and items. An individual user may have multiple responsibilities. Design considerations must be made to determine whether all elements of the multiple responsibilities will be displayed on the individual portal page, distributed to multiple pages based on responsibilities, or controlled by forcing a single responsibility to be selected at any one time. Another key element of portal security is the development of a single sign-on and authentication mechanism. Much of the ease of use within a portal framework disappears if users are required to log in to multiple applications within the portal. Security planning also must consider what access will be provided to users exclusively within the campus Intranet environment and what elements will be made available to portal users through Internet access. Although the goal for Santa Barbara City College is clearly "anytime, anywhere" access to campus information, product licensing and campus network security may often dictate limitation to access only while on campus.

Availability and Support

Another key planning dimension is to assess the need for ongoing support and sustainability of the portal environment. This operational planning has several components. First, support and maintenance of portal hardware and software must be considered. Any components of the portal framework that are made available over the Internet must be supported on a "7 by 24 by 365" basis. There is no excused downtime, no set hours of operation, and no patience for system failures. At Santa Barbara City College, this lesson was learned quickly as we developed our Online College offerings. In the first year of operation of the Online College, with a very limited number of courses offered, the "off-hour" demands on our Web master and user support staff were tremendous. During the second year of operation, the Online College contracted with a local Internet service provider for hardware, operating system, and help-desk support for the seventy courses offered. In the third year of operation, we contracted with Sprint Corporation's Web Hosting Services to add the Campus Pipeline student portal server to the WebCT server hosting the Online College course content for more than a hundred courses. This year the college is adding an iPlanet messaging and calendaring server to the student portal, and also adding firewall security at the hosted site to serve in conjunction with the existing campus firewall. This portal framework will serve more than 130 course offerings and five thousand students. Whereas Sprint is providing around-the-clock support for the hardware, operating system, and network connectivity, the database and application level support are still the responsibility of, and managed by, the college.

Training

No portal implementation can achieve success without proper training of the college community on the structure, navigation, tools, content, and uses of the Intranet site. At Santa Barbara City College this training component includes presentations by the office of institutional assessment, research, and planning, the faculty resource center, the staff resource center, and the information resources division. The role of the office of institutional assessment, research, and planning is essential, in that it provides campus training on data structures, ad hoc query capabilities, analytical tools, and reporting. We have found that the most successful training is tied directly to the job requirements of the individual or group to be trained. Generic vendor training on a particular analysis tool, for example, is rarely sustainable when individuals return to their desks, because there is no structure for the immediate use and reinforcement of the training in a real-life situation. Our training modules have had far more success when designed around a departmental-specific analysis or task to be accomplished.

Project Staffing

The design, development, and implementation of a campus Intranet portal are significant undertakings for any institution. Both the time and resources that need to be committed to the project are precious commodities within higher education institutions. The challenges are particularly acute for community colleges and smaller four-year institutions that often lack the technology infrastructure and support mechanisms required for large-scale technology deployments. As in most human endeavors, however, good people working together in a focused way can accomplish much. At Santa Barbara City College the Intranet development team consisted of the following roles: project manager (one), institutional researcher (one), Web developer (one), database administrator (one), functional specialists (six), and trainers (two). This core development team worked to develop the initial prototype of the college Intranet portal presented to the college cabinet and management team. The group then began to fill in content for the production version of the portal. We brought in additional Web content developers from departmental staff as each new area was added to the production version of the portal. Just-in-time training was provided to the content developers in order for them to be ready to maintain content on an ongoing basis. The office of institutional assessment, research, and planning provided training to academic deans in decision-support tools and data. The working group developed the initial prototype in a month, whereas the additional specification of the production portal was a three-month project. We are now in a year-long project to complete the campus Intranet portal content and to move the service into ongoing maintenance and support.

Campus Portal Planning and Implementation

When beginning the implementation of a portal one of the most important considerations is to understand that the institution must have a long-term commitment to the project. A portal, by its dynamic nature, is never finished. As technology and the needs of the organization and individuals change, the portal must "morph" to meet the new demands. A portal that does not have this flexibility (and dedication to ongoing support and maintenance) is doomed. Like any major technology project, a significant institutional investment in planning and design of the institution's portal is an important first step toward a successful implementation.

Conclusion

There are a few points from the chapter that deserve to be reinforced in conclusion. First, the development of systems, content, and processes for *personalized content delivery* is essential for a successful implementation of an institutional portal. This objective should drive decisions concerning design, content, format, and tools to be used within the portal framework. The portal must be relevant and rewarding to individuals in their respective roles within the organization. Second, *decentralization of Web content* development and maintenance is a key objective for ongoing sustainability and support of an institutional portal. This is especially important for community colleges and smaller four-year institutions, and can be achieved through the development and training of departmental staff on institutional templates and resource libraries, stored in a central database repository. A formal training program for departmental Web developers is also a key success factor in this area. Third, the use of robust search engines provides a far more effective vehicle for document retrieval and management that relying on the navigation of hierarchical file folders or organizational taxonomies. *Rapid full-text search and weighting of all documents* (regardless of type) provide the most sustainable, flexible, and useful retrieval capabilities.

Finally, in a publication targeted to institutional researchers, a chapter written by institutional chief technology officers may be suspect. We would like to reiterate, however, our vision of the *central role played by institutional research* within the development of higher education portals. At Santa Barbara City College, the office of institutional assessment, research, and planning is driving the design and development of the institutional portal to implement a new decision-support system. We have pointed out the significantly expanded role this has meant for the institutional research function within the college in terms of database design, policy development, Web content development, training, and technology infrastructure planning. This expansion of responsibilities may be viewed skeptically by some in the profession but is a rather natural outcome of placing improved institutional decision making at the heart of higher education Intranet portal strategies.

References

Borck, J. R. *Next-Generation Portals,* 2001. [http://iwsun4.infoworld.com/articles/op/xml/01/06/11/010611opborck.xml].

Di Maio, A. *Why Today's Government Portals Are Irrelevant.* Stamford, Conn.: Gartner Group, January 2001.

Harris, K., and Caldwell, F. "Knowledge Management Scenario: The Enterprise and Beyond." Paper presented at the Gartner Symposium ITXPO, Orlando, Fla., October 11–16, 2000.

Hayward, S. "Choosing Wisely: Technology for Knowledge Management." Paper presented at the Gartner Symposium ITXPO, Orlando, Fla., October 11–16, 2000.

Internet Software Consortium. *Internet Domain Survey,* January 2001. [http://www.isc.org/ds/WWW-200101/index.html].

Moore, C. *Portal Power,* 2001. [http://iwsun4.infoworld.com/articles/fe/xml/01/06/11/010611feknowledge.xml].

Phifer, G., and Zastrocky, M. *Best Practices in Deploying Institution-Wide Portals.* Stamford, Conn.: Gartner Group, August 2, 2000.

Roueche, J. E., Ely, E. E., and Roueche, S. D. "Challenges of the Heart: Pursuing Excellence at the Community College of Denver." *Community College Journal,* Dec.–Jan. 2001, pp. 30–34.

Rudy, J. "Campus Profile: Santa Barbara City College." *CAUSE/EFFECT,* Winter 1996, *19*(4), 32–35.

Ryland, J. N. *Technology and the Future of the Community College.* New Expeditions, Issues Paper No. 10. Washington, D.C.: American Association of Community Colleges, 2000.

Yanosky, R. *Higher Education Enterprise Portals: Profiles of an Emerging Provider Class.* Stamford, Conn.: Gartner Group, March 3, 2000.

RICHARD PICKETT is executive director of technical marketing at Oracle Corporation.

WILLIAM HAMRE is vice president of the information resource division at Santa Barbara City College.

4

The thrusts of customer relationship management are improved customer tracking, understanding, and responsiveness. In an environment where competition for students, dollars, and teaching talent is increasingly fierce, a well-designed and well-utilized customer relationship management infrastructure provides the means for better customer interaction and service and represents an important link in the knowledge management chain.

Customer Relationship Management

Michael Fayerman

What comes to mind when we hear the words *customer, customer loyalty,* and *competition?* Usually it is an image associated with the world of business competition such an advertising campaign or a television commercial. During the last decade, the same forces driving dramatic changes in business, the Internet, customer-centered cultures, and globalization have also had an impact on the world of colleges and universities. Today, higher education institutions face the same challenges experienced in the private sector. Just as the New Economy consumer is accustomed to personalized and high-quality customer service, today's consumers of higher education have higher expectations than even five years ago. Increased competition for students, fundraising dollars, and teaching talent impels higher education leaders to reevaluate existing business practices and differentiate themselves from the rest. It is against such background that this chapter addresses the needs and outlines the methods by which customer relationship management can be applied in higher education institutions with assistance from institutional research professionals.

In the pre-Y2K era, colleges and universities focused on improving back-office operations by conducting system integration, business process reengineering, and enterprise resource planning (ERP) implementations. These efforts resulted in a solid technological infrastructure and rich databases. Now it is time for higher education institutions to further break down departmental barriers, leverage operational improvements, and focus on developing stronger relationships with their customers. The word *customer* is used throughout this chapter to maintain connection to customer relationship management, but it is not my intent to insist on regarding all personnel in a higher education setting as customers.

Colleges and universities have many customers to consider, including current, former, and prospective students, parents, faculty, staff, government organizations, vendors, corporate sponsors, and the community at large. These customers may be grouped into three categories: consumers, business to business customers, and internal customers. Each customer type interacts with a different functional area or areas of a college or university. Knowing customer interests, identified via historical records, can enhance the interactions and overall relationships higher education institutions have with their customers. Transforming a customer's historical information into customer knowledge can further benefit customers and higher education institutions alike. The process and technology that can translate customer information into customer knowledge is called *customer relationship management* (CRM). Recent technical innovations have made CRM a reliable, affordable, and implementable technology.

Customer Relationship Management: Definition and Processes

CRM's strength lies in its required foundation: robust databases, network speed, ERP automation of back office functions, Internet acceptance, and communication technology. CRM is an enterprisewide business strategy designed to optimize revenue and customer satisfaction by organizing the institution around customer segments. This strategy may represent a serious change in the existing organizational culture and behavior. The resulting transformation allows organizations to more effectively select, attract, retain, and even grow customers. Part technology solution, part process design, CRM encourages symbiotic relationships between customers and colleges, as well as within the higher education institution itself. Automation plays an important part in this strategy, as does institutionwide integration such as knowledge management, data warehousing, data mining, front office technology, and organizational portals.

On one level, CRM provides colleges and universities a clear and complete picture of each individual customer and all activities pertaining to that customer within the institution. On another level, CRM allows customers to interact with the college or university as a single entity by providing customers a clear understanding of their status within the organization. For a student, this might include information regarding admissions, registration, financial aid, student accounts, and housing.

Peppers and Rogers (1999) see the difference between the CRM process and traditional database marketing determined by four key actions: identify, differentiate, interact, and customize. As they explain it: "The difference is about customization—about generating feedback from customers so that marketers can learn more about their preferences, so future offers of products, packaging, delivery, communications, or even invoicing can be tailored to these preferences." This approach, with its focus on individualized service delivery, serves as one of the most significant components of CRM's theoretical framework.

Consulting firms, such as KPMG Consulting, regularly help colleges and universities apply CRM to one customer in particular: the next incoming class of students. For this target group, CRM is used to develop strategy and architecture to create personalized communication and custom activities. Once the prospective student enrolls, the institution can leverage the combined power of the student and financial systems, personalization software, and data warehouse toward simplified access and review of transcripts, tuition, and billing history.

Another successful application of CRM in colleges and universities is in educational advancement. It enhances the interaction with alumni and donors during all phases and activities of fundraising, stewardship, and alumni relations by applying customized and targeted information to the customer through appropriate contact mechanisms.

Building upon one-to-one marketing and one-to-one servicing concepts, CRM allows

- Selective targeting of those individuals within the donor pool identified, through research, as having the highest probability of giving
- Customized mass mailing (that is, direct mail) materials to be sent to prospects
- Management of all interactions from solicitation through stewardship and ongoing sponsorship by the account center (that is, gift processing)
- Scripting for prompt consistent answers to inquiries
- Profiling for proactive service to build alumni loyalty

The benefits of applying CRM in educational advancement are increased effectiveness of campaigns and solicitations, increased average amount of donations, increased customer satisfaction, reduced campaign cost, and increased alumni participation. Berry and Linoff (2000) discussed these types of benefits extensively.

As mentioned above, CRM provides a single point of contact for a college or university's customers. In the example of a student, not only will that individual have access to his or her admissions, financial, or academic status, but also the student will have multiple ways to access this varied information. CRM provides students (and their parents) with the means to control the service they receive. Customers can choose the mode or channel of interaction (Web, e-mail, in-person, fax, and so forth) at any time. These channels are integrated so that customers can move freely through and between channels. For example, a student may make a service request via the Internet in the morning, fax back-up documentation an hour later, e-mail a correction after lunch, and call to check on the request's status later in the afternoon. If the student chooses to stop by the administrative

office in person to check on the request's status, the customer service officer will have electronic access not only to those contacts the student had
made earlier in the day but also to the information the student had
requested. Both student and service representative will benefit from the
high-quality, efficient system of information transfer and retrieval the CRM
software can provide.

Establishing a CRM Strategy

Few institutions would want to devote enough resources and political support to embark on CRM without first devising a plan based on vision. To
begin the CRM journey, colleges and universities need to create a clear vision
of their CRM strategy, including the necessary steps toward the project's successful implementation. There are five recommended activities in creating
an effective CRM strategy (Meta Group, 1999):

1. Identify information and interaction process flows between the customer and your educational institution.
2. Integrate customer service functions.
3. Transition from reactive to proactive customer service knowledge.
4. Shift to a customer-centered organization.
5. Measure success and value over time.

The successful CRM strategy must include effective use of data integration technology such as knowledge management, data warehousing,
sophisticated delivery channel systems, and analytics. The key elements of
the CRM strategy include customer information architecture that ensures
accurate and integrated customer information. The best approach is the
development of a customer data warehouse, as well as delivery channels
such as campaign management tools and customer service applications.
Collaborative architecture further ensures a single point of contact through
organizational portals and analytical systems that enable decision makers to
analyze customer information.

Prudent institutions view information across the organization via
development of an institutionwide data model. The institutionwide data
model depicts a consolidated view of the organization so all customer relationships collected from multiple systems can be viewed consistently and
accurately. For a long time, colleges and universities have treated customer
data as many separate silos, with separate, often disparate, sources of information for each customer in multiple databases. The goal of a CRM installation is to capture all this information—from admissions data to financial
aid statements to registration status—and manage it appropriately. Effective
management of this information requires storage in easy-to-retrieve structures that allow both customers and CRM users instant access and an
instant view to all necessary, available data when the customer interacts

with the organization. To accomplish this goal, CRM is linked with knowledge management, a process that requires digitalization of the full customer interaction life cycle.

In its ideal form, CRM will become a systemic approach to customer life cycle management (CLCM). CLCM is a three-domain business system, aligning business processes, technologies, and the customer life cycle (Meta Group, 2000). The business system must integrate customer acquisition, service, and marketing processes and the CRM technology environment with the customer and then be organized into the CRM technology ecosystem (Meta Group, 2000). To fully realize the potential of CRM, this business system must be synchronized with the customer life cycle (CLC), which is dependent on the customer in consideration.

Meta Group (2000) defines *customer life cycle* as a pattern consisting of four elements: engage, transact, fulfill, service (ETFS).

- *Stage 1: engage.* The initial customer awareness of the institution is created via advertising or marketing activities. This creates basic awareness, which results in a customer interaction with the institution, be it prospective students applying to the college or university or alumni expressing interest in making a donation to their alma mater.
- *Stage 2: transact.* The actual transaction occurs, such as a student registering for a course or an alumnus sending in a donation.
- *Stage 3: fulfill.* The customer transaction is complemented by an institutional response, be it a student being registered for and attending a particular course, or an alumnus receiving a gift receipt and thank you note for the donation.
- *Stage 4: service.* The institution continues to support its customers, including students and alumni, by providing information, processing information, or resolving issues on an ongoing basis.

The CRM Ecosystem

The CRM ecosystem is a component-based application that automates customer-related business processes. The components of the CRM ecosystem are presented in Figure 4.1. The major components of a CRM ecosystem are the operational CRM, the analytical CRM, and the collaborative CRM, explained below.

Operational CRM. Operational CRM involves the automation of horizontally integrated business processes involving front-office customer touch points including marketing, recruiting, and customer service and back-office applications such as human resources, financial, student, alumni, and fundraising systems. This core CRM operational portfolio includes lead and opportunity management and a call center–customer interaction center. However, the human resources, financial, student, and other operational systems include information necessary for CRM. Many ERP vendors are entering the CRM market either by acquiring or building

Figure 4.1. CRM Ecosystem

Operational CRM   *Analytical CRM*

Back office	HR and financial systems	Student, alumni, and fundraising systems	Other legacy systems		Data warehouse

Closed-loop processing (EAI toolkits, embedded mobile agents)

Front office	Marketing automation	Recruiting automation	Service automation	Customer activity data mart	Customer data mart	Enterprise data mart

Mobile office		Mobile recruiting	Mobile service	Vertical apps / Category management	Marketing automation / Campaign management

Customer interaction	Voice (IVR, ACD)	Web / Web conferencing	e-Mail / Resp management	Fax, letter	Direct interaction

Collaborative CRM

Source: Meta Group and KPMG Consulting.

CRM capabilities. Oracle and Peoplesoft-Vantive are considered strong in the sales and service function of operational CRM. By using an end-to-end vendor for CRM as part of an ERP suite with financial, student, and human resource modules, the institution will achieve integration more effectively and efficiently. However, vendors such as Siebel offer more out-of-the-box functionality and may better address institutions' customer management requirements.

Analytical CRM. The analysis of data created in the operational component of the ecosystem allows for information consolidation toward definition of customer behavior. The analytical component is usually created around a data warehouse that feeds various analytical applications and data marts. The purpose of the analytical CRM component is to develop a panoramic view of the customer. Failure to develop this component will jeopardize the effectiveness of an institution's CRM efforts. Institutional researchers can greatly benefit from a well-designed analytical CRM, which should provide them the explicit knowledge base to conduct sound research on the various customers of an institution.

Collaborative CRM. The application of collaborative interfaces facilitates interaction between customers and institutions. This includes e-mail, interactive voice response systems, Web conferencing, and Web portals.

Portals play an important role in CRM by providing the customer with a single point of contact and a 360 degree view of the institution. Multiple portal views need to exist to fulfill the needs of various constituencies. For example alumni, students, employees, and even parents should have their own individualized portals. Ultimately, the portal view should be customizable by the individual by using a strategy similar to that employed by my.yahoo.com, for example. However, both general customer type and personalized portals should exist within an overall institutional portal model. Colleges and universities can use portals as effective hubs for community-building efforts. As discussed in Chapter Three, collaborative services such as discussion forums can help individuals interact around the information they find valuable on the portal site (Meta Group, 2000).

Though a main component of CRM is Web based, colleges and universities must also consider channel integration and migrate low-value-added tasks and interactions to lower-cost channels when building a CRM strategy. The Internet can serve as an integration mechanism for recruitment and servicing by providing a single point of contact. The e-channel creates opportunities for institutions to deliver self-service directly to customers. Institutions with successfully implemented CRM share a focus on multi-channel CRM initiatives, including face-to-face, call-center, partner, and electronic channels.

The integration of the technology that supports the CRM ecosystem may be very expensive and thus financially prohibitive until institutions have several, individually installed segments of ecosystem in place. At present, most organizations are not pursuing the integration of CRM components on the institutionwide level (Meta Group, 2001). However, it is expected that increased ecosystem integration will become more prevalent over time. According to a Meta Group survey (Meta Group, 2001), 60 percent of respondents reported some level of integration in progress. The trend is most likely going to hold, if not increase.

Several institutions that implemented Oracle and Peoplesoft ERP systems are beginning to explore greater integration of CRM components. Other institutions are applying campaign management tools and portals as entry point to CRM. In July 1999, a major midwestern university conducted a comprehensive phone and mail survey of its alumni. Almost 50 percent of respondents wanted regular updates via e-mail or the university's Web site. The university moved forward with developing the alumni portal. The portal provides an easy way for the university to gather alumni information and stay in contact with their alumni. As the university began collecting information about alumni through the portal's profile section, they took a step further by developing personalized e-newsletters by using Liquid Matrix software. Now the university can automatically customize e-mail newsletters based on the alumnus profile. The software allows the university to code news stories in the database. Stories are targeted by graduation date, geographic location, and other profiling criteria and electronically delivered to more than seven thousand individuals in less than half an hour.

The university uses customer segmentation techniques to develop stories based on interest. For example, sport buffs receive stories on the university's sport teams. If alumni have not made the donation, they are encouraged to do so. If they donate, they receive a personalized story thanking them.

The initial three newsletters received almost six thousand click-throughs to news stories and other university links. The university is not planning to eliminate traditional channels and is interested in integrating them with the Web strategy. The alumnus portal drives traffic to other locations such as the bookstore and the reunion site. This architecture thus promotes cross-selling. In addition, the university estimated savings of $18 thousand per year from not having to mail address-update postcards. Before developing the alumnus portal and e-newsletter, only 13 percent of alumni donated; after the technology was introduced the rate increased to 30 percent. The e-newsletter approach is not unique, but most institutions do not apply personalization to them. In the future, the university plans to distinguish alumni based on donor level and to expand its strategy. They envision using this technology not just to attract more donor money but also to spread the word about the university and develop a linkage between alumni and admissions.

Making the customer the central design point is one of the critical elements of CRM. Many organizations organize their technology efforts around a function or product. To achieve a true customer-centered state, colleges and universities must design their business processes and technology systems around the customer and around the customer life cycle and ultimately the integration of all components of the CRM's ecosystem. As with portals, CRM does not start with technology, it starts with philosophy and reevaluation of the organization's culture. This requires a fundamental shift in traditional industry philosophy, cooperation of all participants, and inclusion of ideas that have been rarely used before in the organization (Swift, 2001). For example, the marketing unit needs to agree to share extraction of data and marketing techniques with other departments. Only true open communication and joint sponsorship among colleges' and universities' different business units can ensure the transition to a customer-centered organization. The customer will realize that the organization is addressing their needs by being flexible and responsive.

The Role of a Program Management Office in CRM Implementations

As organizations establish enterprisewide customer relationship management initiatives, CRM-specific program management is key to creating successful, customer-centered CRM implementations. The creation of a program management office (PMO) can help CRM implementations. Similar to the working group described in the previous chapter that Santa Barbara City College created for the implementation of its portal, this is not an information technology (IT) or a functional entity. The PMO should include representatives from financial, human resources, marketing, institutional advancement, institutional research, and other departments. Such inclusiveness is particularly important to bridge the schism between IT organizations and functional units and also to better incorporate actual customer needs with available CRM technology and skill sets. The PMO's goal is to effectively coordinate projects, including key milestones, budgets, and dependencies, across the organization. The CRM program director works with the project managers to implement the overall CRM program and also coordinates the overall program. The project manager coordinates best practices and process integration. These roles work together across major CRM project initiatives, including data warehousing, conversions and interfaces, CRM package selection and implementation, and sales automation.

In addition to coordinating customer requirements, the PMO drives requirements of the CRM framework and architecture, as well as the business process architecture, and coordinates with the ETFS (engage, transact, fulfill, and service) cycle to establish the overall CRM ecosystem. Once all the processes are defined and it becomes clear what the ecosystem looks like, a CRM software can be selected. Regularly established meetings and accountability to the PMO for key milestones and progression of project dependencies such as budget and scheduling remain critical throughout the duration of the CRM initiative (Meta Group, 2001). Institutional researchers can play a critical role in a PMO by providing insights into the type of data warehouse that would best capture the elements needed for analyses and research targeted on understanding institutional customers and their behaviors outside the institution.

To a large extent, barriers to establishing an effective CRM PMO continue to be cultural and political. However, the complexity of institutionwide CRM initiatives and the success of program-specific organizational strategies are now driving upper management to establish strong CRM PMOs. In addition, the importance of coordinating resource allocation for CRM PMOs with other initiatives such as ERP is further driving the impetus for establishment of an institutionwide PMO to coordinate cross-program implementation. This is important not only for the more efficient functioning of program implementation, but also for establishing effective strategies for rolling out multiple initiatives to the user community. Coordination of key corporate initiatives such as CRM, ERP, and e-commerce, which directly affect end-user productivity and business success, must be well coordinated or the initiatives will fail at the release stage. Therefore, colleges and universities with institutionwide CRM initiatives are advised to establish a PMO office.

CRM and Institutional Research

"CRM is not just about automating tasks. Companies are demanding a deeper level of understanding of their customers" (Yeaman, 2001). The understanding of customers is the realm of the analytical CRM. As an SPSS executive points out, "Analytical CRM isn't really for everybody. You have to have a product or service where knowing [the customer] makes a difference, and gives you some kind of advantage that will make you work smarter or better and please customers" (cited in Compton, 2001). In other words, by itself the implementation of a CRM infrastructure will achieve little if all the data gathered are not analyzed, understood, and put into context (transformed into information) and if patterns are not identified (transformed to knowledge) and, finally, translated into action. CRM has the capability to be a critical component of knowledge management as long as an institution has the analytical tools and staff with the expertise to delve into the massive amounts of data stored in CRM databases. Closing the distance between customer data and customer understanding is an analytical CRM tool being offered by everyone from traditional operational CRM providers to upstarts to long-term data mining specialists (Compton, 2001).

By the nature of the trade, institutional researchers have the analytical and technical skills, or could further enhance them, to be able to take advantage of the potential offered by CRM infrastructures. As mentioned earlier, although the operational and collaborative CRM components benefit mostly functional units such as admissions, institutional advancement, and alumni relations, the analytical component could remain largely underutilized without the involvement and expertise of institutional research staff. Institutional researchers have already frequently conducted studies related to prospective students and alumni, for example. However, the significant difference between the traditional research conducted for segments of customers, where researchers would start with analyzing existing data on a given customer segment as a means of making predictions for others in the same segment, CRM allows—through the use of data mining techniques, for example—the identification of affinity groups, which in turn leads to a better understanding of the customers and the interplay between customer characteristics and customers' use of services. An application of this approach could be identifying patterns within the characteristics of customers of student services such as counseling, career centers, health and wellness, and others. By tapping into the data gathered through CRM, institutional researchers could make analytical insights and results available to a broad range of functional users who can then improve their customer related strategies and could support activities such as unit program reviews.

Conclusion

Although CRM has been used by many businesses for a number of years, it is yet to gain widespread acceptance in higher education primarily due to the cost and resources required for successful implementation and deployment. However, as mentioned earlier, campuses that have implemented CRM have already seen some of its benefits through increased customer responsiveness and satisfaction.

From a knowledge management perspective, CRM represents one of the links needed for better understanding of organizational customers and for providing the means to achieve competitive advantage through improved customer tracking and responsiveness. A key strength of CRM lies in its analytical component, which institutional researchers are best suited to manage.

References

Berry, M., and Linoff, G. *Master Data Mining: The Art and Science of Customer Relationship Management.* New York: Wiley Computer Publishing, 2000.

Compton, J. "Number Crunching for Customer Understanding." *CRM Magazine,* Oct. 2001. [http://www.destinationcrm.com/cr/dcrm_cr_article.asp?id=711].

Meta Group. *CRM Ecosystem.* Stamford, Conn.: Meta Group, 2000.

Meta Group. *CRM Ecosystem.* Stamford, Conn.: Meta Group, 2001.

Peppers, D., and Rogers, M. *The One-to-One Manager: An Executive's Guide to Customer Relationship Management.* New York: Random House, 1999.

Swift, R. S. *Accelerating Customer Management.* New Jersey: Prentice Hall, 2001.

Yeaman, K. "The Brains of the Operation" *CRM Magazine,* June 2001. [http://www.destinationcrm.com/cr/dcrm_cr_article.asp?id=632].

MICHAEL FAYERMAN is senior manager in the higher education division of KPMG Consulting, Inc., in New York.

For knowledge management to be successful, organizational learning and a research culture must support it. This chapter presents various models of organizational learning as they influence the design and implementation of knowledge-based systems. The theoretical considerations presented are exemplified by a discussion of the impact of accountability movements on higher education, in general, and institutional research, in particular, and on the creation and implementation of knowledge-based systems in colleges and universities.

Organizational Learning and the Case for Knowledge-Based Systems

Lisa A. Petrides

Using technology to provide information to decision makers has proven to be a more difficult task in the education sector, partly as a result of a lack of financial resources available for technology infrastructure and support and partly because higher education institutions have not traditionally been under the same pressure as business institutions to become self-sustaining and profitable. However, as the current accountability movement has spread across the country, there has been a growing need for reliable internal and external information (Wells, Silk, and Torres, 1999).

Many institutions have a desire for research that informs their decision making, but the lack of technical infrastructure has seemingly thwarted their efforts. In addition, numerous studies have shown that technology tools alone do not address issues of organizational cultures and structures (Telem, 1996; Sirotnik and Burstein, 1987). Instead, the adaptation of technology must be embedded within organizational processes in an iterative process of trial and experimentation (Levine, 2001). However, it is much easier to persuade organizations to acquire new technology tools than to modify or redesign existing processes within the organization (Coate, 1996). Many failed information system implementations in higher education have been attributed to an unmet need on the part of the organization to address issues of information sharing and knowledge creation from multiple viewpoints (Leonard and Straus, 1997; Levine, 2001). Others have spoken to the information politics within an organization as likely causes of information system failure (Davenport, 1997; Friedman and Hoffman, 2001; Petrides, Khanuja-Dhall, and Reguerin, 2000).

As noted in the opening chapter, businesses have become increasingly concerned with mobilizing what they believe is their greatest asset, knowledge: the combination of information, experience, circumstances, and understanding that can be applied to any decisions or situations (Cliffe, 1998; Hansen, Nohria, and Tierney, 1999; Zisman, 1999; Davenport, 1997). Managing knowledge networks within organizations has now become a critical challenge taken up by the business community (Zisman, 1999). Business and some education organizations are increasingly moving toward models of organizational learning that are based on knowledge-driven decision making.

Various authors suggest that organizational transformation will occur only if the process itself is knowledge-driven and if members of the educational learning community develop and implement knowledge-based systems (COIL, 1999; Bloodgood and Salisbury, 2001). So whereas in the early 1990s knowledge management practices focused primarily on the management of existing data-based resources within an organization, today the focus on knowledge management has been to help identify additional information needs throughout the organization and then to use innovative information technology tools to create, capture, and use that information to meet organizational goals (Duffy, 2000). Knowledge management today is described as a process in which knowledge is created as a result of the multidimensional categorization of information in several different contexts by multiple users (Duffy, 2000; Levine, 2001). However, the implementation of knowledge management practices varies a great deal across organizations.

Knowledge Management from an Organizational Learning Perspective

The evolution from data to information and from information to knowledge has played a leading role in shaping how organizations develop strategies and plans for the future. Several authors believe that successful organizations that forge ahead in a rapidly changing business environment will do so through the creating and sharing of new knowledge (Argyris and Schon, 1996; Senge, 1997; Brown, 1999; Senge, 1990). The use of cross-functional teams, customer or product-focused business units and work groups, and communities of practice are just a few of the emerging trends that allow organizations to make the best use of their most valuable asset, their staff (Sveiby, 1997; Brown, 1999). Thus, organizational learning from a knowledge management perspective provides the opportunity for the goals and objectives of the organization to be cultivated simultaneously with the goals and objectives of the individual (COIL, 1999). Specifically, this means that people are important to the learning process within the organization but organizational learning cannot be reduced to individual learning (Levine, 2001).

Within an organizational learning context, an ecological approach to knowledge management has been explored by Thomas Davenport's work on information ecology, which calls for communities of practice to be involved in the establishment of an ecological model that is holistically managed within an organization. The human-centered information management model described by Davenport focuses on the information environment, the organizational environment that surrounds it, and the external environment of the marketplace. In this model, primary importance is placed on the people within the organization, in terms of their strategic use of information, information politics, and the culture and behavior of individuals within an organization (Davenport, 1997).

An ecological approach to knowledge management is based on the assumption that the accumulation of data is influenced by the core values of the college or university (or a group or team or department within the institution), and that through some process of human interaction and context, including the use of computers to access and review the data, these data then take on significance and importance as information. Next, through the process of context, accumulation of data, sense making, synthesis, and reflection, this information is transformed and converted to knowledge that is relevant to decision making within the organization, which then may or may not produce an action step but does influence the next round of data accumulation (Brown, Collins, and Duguid, 1989; COIL, 1999; Johnson, 1996). For example, it might be that the use of information may change the organization in terms of producing more effective decision making, or that a transformation occurs within the organizational structure in the process of using the information itself.

Another ecological model, the knowledge ecology model, has at its core an active, interdependent, and complex adaptive system that adds an innately systemic dimension to the knowledge and learning that occurs within the community (COIL, 1999; Brown, 2000; Sveiby, 1997). Within a knowledge ecology perspective is the accrued expertise and learning within the ecosystem, where ideas are exchanged, innovation blossoms, and value is added to information, thus producing new knowledge to test and apply in the internal and external environment, predominantly through the use of information systems (COIL, 1999).

What Are Knowledge-Based Systems?

Approaches to knowledge management, which vary across the data-information-knowledge continuum, affect the design and implementation of knowledge-based systems. At one end of the continuum is the building of data-based information systems that seek to capture the knowledge of those within the organization and make it available to the organization as a whole (Brown, 2000; Mitchell, 2000). This includes decision support systems that allow users to extract useful information in large datasets in order to run analyses that support decision-making efforts within the organization. It also includes the use of data mining, which has been addressed in Chapter Two. The primary focus in using knowledge management for data-based information systems is to systematically manage, leverage, and store knowledge within an organization (Laudon and Laudon, 2001). This can include the creation and sharing of both internal and external knowledge. Most data-based information systems contain quantitative elements that lack the value-added tacit qualities of information (Davenport, 1997). At the other end of the spectrum is an approach to knowledge management that includes building and managing systems that are knowledge-based. These systems are designed through an ongoing course of action that examines the work processes and technical systems as well as changes in social and behavioral aspects of work, such as culture, group dynamics, and collaboration (Davenport, DeLong, and Beers, 1998; Levine, 2001). Bernbom (1999) suggests that institutional researchers assess their information management practices as a way to understand both the formal and informal information environment of the institution, thereby helping facilitate interconnections among different data sources within their institutions. In this way, the institutional researcher becomes a knowledge industry analyst who is involved in all levels of institutional information and services (Peterson, 1999).

Knowledge-based systems are in fact an outgrowth of an ecological model of knowledge management, which deliberately uses a sociotechnical approach to managing information systems that combine organizational processes with the use of innovative technology in knowledge management practices (Telem, 1996; Levine, 2001). This approach has also been referred to as technology change management, in which organizational changes that are necessary to implement and maintain successful knowledge management systems are made explicit through the advent of organizational learning (Levine, 2001). Equally as important is the sharing of internal tacit knowledge, which was defined in Chapter One.

The purpose of having knowledge-based systems is to be able to make more informed, research-driven policies and procedures that improve program and service delivery to students as well as to faculty, staff, and administration within the organization. The ongoing and iterative process of design, implementation, and feedback that takes place within these knowledge-based systems is the hallmark knowledge management from an organizational learning perspective. Essentially, associations of people create knowledge systems that are supported and elevated by technology networks, where all members of the organization have expertise not only in managing information and knowledge-based systems, but also in assessing and taking action to promote organizational change in terms of educational management, attitudes, organizational behavior, and policy. Thus, as higher education institutions implement and maintain knowledge-based systems, they are likely to see structural, political, human, and symbolic modifications within the organization.

Creation of Knowledge-Based Systems

As mentioned earlier, the creation of knowledge-based systems is an ongoing iterative process that involves not only the planners and designers of these systems but also end-users of information throughout the organization. The underlying motivation for creating knowledge-based systems is to understand how organizations can become better at what they do by using internal and external information systems to support a cycle of continuous learning (Argyris, 1991; COIL, 1999; Garvin, 1993). At the core of the continuous learning system is an ecological approach to knowledge management. This ecological approach is not based on solving a particular problem per se. The purpose is to support a culture of research and inquiry that informs continuous improvement of an organization's mission and goals on an ongoing basis. This allows the needs of research to determine the direction of the development of information systems, as opposed to the more common approach that lets the information system dictate the needs of research based on a centrally prescribed set of outputs. Hence, a knowledge-based system does more than just support decision making; it is also about a process that enables an organization to decide on an ongoing basis what the problems are. This is also referred to as double-loop learning, which asks not just questions about what the problems are, but the reasons and motives behind those questions (Friedman and Hoffman, 2001; Morgan, 1986; Levine, 2001).

Four key elements have been identified as central to the process of creating knowledge-based systems: (1) the identification of information strategies, (2) an ongoing awareness of the organizational context, (3) an examination of information politics within the organization, and (4) an assessment of the external environment and its influence on information needs. I discuss each one in more detail in what follows, and give examples for each of the four elements to illustrate their relatedness to the creation of knowledge-based systems in higher education, with implications for institutional research and planning.

Information Strategies. Articulated mission and goals enable organizations to develop strategic planning. It is equally important to clearly tie organizational information needs to those missions and goals and to identify the type of information that is needed to support decision-making and policies that are in line with the goal and mission of the organization (Drucker, 1988). This can be based on well-defined problems, as well as through pattern-seeking strategies such as data mining. For example, if student success is the mission, and increasing the number of minority students who major in math and science is a goal, then the information needs would focus on demographic, enrollment, and program data. Alternatively, if the goal is to have graduate students finish their education in five years or less, then an alternative information strategy might be to collect and analyze data on graduate student attrition, departmental support, and financial aid. If a college is trying to make informed decisions about student services that will positively impact student success, then information on those programs and services is needed instead.

There may be multiple information needs throughout an organization, but linking them specifically to the overall mission and goals of the organization is essential to the successful design, implementation, and actual use of information systems (Drucker, 1988; Laudon and Laudon, 2001). For example, data-gathering processes might require individual requests to be made, data to be extracted, and individual analyses to be conducted, often by people who are uncertain of the information and its intended purpose. In addition, whether or not information needs and strategies are openly discussed in the organization is also important (Walleri and Stoering, 1996). Information strategies in higher education include both the administrative aspects of higher education and instruction. Identifying information needs includes naming the problems that information can resolve, determining what and how much additional information might be required to solve a problem, and then planning for the collection of additional data (Sirotnik and Burstein, 1987).

Organizational Context. Information behavior and culture make up the organizational context for knowledge-based systems (Davenport, 1997; Petrides, Khanuja-Dhall, and Reguerin, 2000). Knowledge-based systems are likely to be more successful if the culture communicates the value and importance of information and knowledge. Organizational learning is likely to take place when work is done within the context of the organization's processes, structure, culture, and human resource issues, which include philosophy and goals, leadership, and cultural assumptions (Schein, 1992). Organizational behavior and culture are embodied by the structures, functions, and norms that support the data-information-knowledge-action cycle (McDermott, 1999). This includes looking at the planning and design process in terms of who is involved, as well as at the technical architecture within the organization, which is important to the flow of knowledge and information within an organization (Davenport, 1997). Ultimately, the acquisition of information by administrators and staff on issues such as resource allocation, scheduling, budgeting, administration, and services creates a feedback loop into the system because of the impact that the information has had on the goals of the organization.

In the case of student success, there could be multiple methods used to aquire student information through various organizational structures, such as making a request to an institutional research office, creating personal databases, or asking colleagues or staff. The effectiveness of decisions based upon information attained via any of these methods can be compromised by a lack of reliability, validity, and congruence of the information. Due to the absence of standard terminology, inconsistent reporting formats and methods, spotty data collection methods, and incomplete records, the same question can result in hundreds of different factual answers, each accurate in its own way. Therefore, an assessment of the type of information that is currently available and the development of a road map that illustrates how information flows throughout the organization will help in understanding information behavior (Davenport, 1997).

Information Politics. There are several key concerns about issues of information politics in the creation of knowledge-based systems. The first is to identify who controls information within the organization and what are the historical reasons for the control within the organization (Davenport, Eccles, and Prusak, 1992). Many institutional research offices are the main repositories of information in higher educational institutions, but those offices can be found under several different places within the organizational structure, such as in departments of planning, instruction, support services, or information technology. Another key question is to determine who provides and interprets the information. If the support services office is the main interpreter of information in terms of written reports and presentations, these interpretations could then be used or discarded by an office of academic instruction because of competition for resources.

Other issues concerning information politics include the sharing of information (Davenport, 1997; McDermott, 1999). As discussed in Chapter One, a key questions is, Are people rewarded for sharing information, whether or not it negatively or positively reflects on a particular program? In many organizations, large amounts of information that could be used for decision making are ignored for this reason (Leonard and Straus, 1997). And finally, it is important to determine whether any type of information sabotage might be going on. This can often be very subtle, such as a database that is not regularly maintained, corrections that are not entered into the system when they are reported, or a duplicate paper version that is maintained in addition to the database information (Davenport, 1997).

External Environment. From an organizational perspective, the external environment is a key element in terms of the need to use external information for internal decision making, as well as for demands for internal information from the external environment. Environmental scanning (for example, demographics of college-age students), competitive analysis (for example, data on who else is competing for an institution's new admissions), and employment data of recent graduates are a few examples of the use of external information for internal decision making. However, there are also external demands for internal information. For example, the accountability movement alone is putting increased demands on public higher education institutions to produce data on student outcomes, such as data about student test scores, persistence, completion, and in the case of two-year colleges, transfer. While the growing concern of state legislatures is primarily with accountability mandates, higher education institutions themselves have a growing need for research that can inform decision making and allow them to assess the effectiveness of their programs independent of the accountability mandates from the state. These demands provide challenges as well as a unique opportunity for higher education institutions to create an environment for organizational learning supported by knowledge-based systems.

Organizational Learning: What Does Institutional Research Have to Do with It?

Similar to the business world, institutions of higher education are looking for ways to apply concepts of organizational learning to help meet their primary goals and objectives. There are several ways in which institutional research offices are well situated to bring organizational learning, facilitated by knowledge management, into the fold of higher education institutions. First, institutional research offices are frequently at the front line of defense in response to accountability mandates, since they are most likely responsible for analysis, interpretation, and dissemination of student outcome data. Second, because institutional research offices have traditionally been the main repository or nucleus of information in colleges and universities, they are likely to encounter a majority of the internal structures and procedures related to the flow of information in the organization. Third, because institutional research has traditionally been the catalyst for internal research and analysis, institutional resource offices are keenly positioned to lend assistance to the creation and maintenance of research-driven decision making. This research-driven decision making is arguably at the core of creating a research culture or culture of inquiry in higher education organizations.

Response to Accountability Mandates

During the 1990s, there was an increase in governmental and public demands for higher education's accountability. In 1997, the state higher education executive officers found that thirty-seven of fifty states used accountability or performance reporting. Since 1995, state accountability objectives have shifted from enhanced learning to demonstrated worth (Nettles and Cole, 1997). In the past, institutions of higher education responded by either complying with minimal reporting standards or directly or indirectly resisting governmental interference in higher education (Ewell, 1994). However, policymakers and the public have become less tolerant of these responses. Concomitantly, there is a growing need for research that can inform decision making and allow the institution to assess the effectiveness of its programs for state mandates and also independently of the accountability mandates from state legislatures.

In the environment of increased demands, there is a shift in institutional research from primarily a reporting function to that of a service function. As a service function, institutional research is in a position to continuously study and assess the institution's programs and serve as a bridge among academic, administrative, and governmental cultures (Volkwein, 1999). However, if institutional research plans to serve in this new role, institutional research staff must have training that, in addition to research skills, includes contextual knowledge and people and facilitation skills (Volkwein, 1999). For example, one college reported that its institutional research staff recently implemented a new process of academic program review. Institutional research staff cooperatively designed and conducted the review with the academic senate. By fusing the academic faculty's interests with the administration's interest, the review was handled efficiently and satisfactorily for both faculty and administration (Petrides, 2001b).

The changing nature of institutional research brings with it unforeseen issues. For instance, mandatory accountability measures compete with other institutional priorities (such as internal reviews) or organizational practices (such as continuous learning models). Institutional research staff in some cases find themselves duplicating efforts by sending information to a central office that will be used to negotiate with state legislatures, but not being able to use the same information for internal needs due to such issues as differing variable definitions or a lack of resources for the institutional research staff (Petrides, 2001b). In addition, accountability potentially creates an environment for campuses that exposes their weaknesses or problem areas, often with fear of punitive measures (Volkwein, 1999).

In the case of one community college faced with outcome-based funding, a tutorial center was given substantial additional funding with the goal of helping contribute to the degree completion rate of its students. The center had previously gathered very little information on students who received their services, other than to find out (often informally) what subjects needed additional tutors. The college administration was very committed to access and equity issues and wanted to ensure that the additional allocation of resources for various programs would be well-spent and provide them a return on their investment in terms of meeting state-mandated outcomes (Petrides, 2001a).

As part of a self-evaluation required for this additional funding, the tutorial center proceeded to create a pre and post questionnaire that students would fill out at the beginning of the semester and again the week before final exams. They created a database that they would use to analyze the data for the semester but also continue to gather and enter data on an ongoing basis. The center had as one of their objectives to increase not only the number of students served, but also to serve those students who were at risk of failing their class, which was in line with the college's equity mission. At the end of the semester, the center discovered that the majority of their students were in fact obtaining A's and B's in their classes and came to the tutorial center regularly in order to maintain their passing grades. The center staff wrote up the self-evaluation and presented it the administration. They were then told that their funding would be curtailed due to the fact that they had not demonstrated that they were meeting the needs of the student population who were at risk of failing a class (the C or D students).

The center staff later went on to successfully lobby the administration to continue their funding based on the premise that they had just collected baseline data and would now be able to make programmatic changes based on their findings. While this was in a sense a productive lesson for the center, it illustrates how a college or university under the stress of meeting state-based mandates may in fact inhibit organizational learning from taking place.

Organizational Learning and Accountability

The combination of organizational learning and accountability mandates may appear at first to be strange bedfellows. However, this intersection can be beneficial to future accountability mandates as well as to the response of higher education institutions if they support a research culture or culture of inquiry, that is, an environment where organizational learning is part of the everyday fabric.

What exactly is a research culture? A research culture is one that purposefully reflects on its own practices by quantitatively and qualitatively studying them and then by creating and implementing alternative actions accordingly (Rallis and MacMullen, 2000). A research culture permeates all levels of the institution and is not reserved for upper level management; it thus transforms all involved players into essential decision makers. Administrators and faculty apply accountability language and processes to new forms of internal improvement and decision making in management as well as in teaching and learning. A research culture involves shifting from a reactive to proactive mode in responding to problems. Reflective inquiry is a model of continuous learning that is a common theme in a research culture. These reflective institutions comprise active professionals who take responsibility for their own work and its subsequent impact and take action in continuous improvement (Argyris, 1991). In a research culture environment, the improvement of teaching and learning is intentional and ongoing. Academic professionals ask questions and collect data that will inform decision making and future action by systematically utilizing data, asking reflective questions, and proceeding with change (Rallis and MacMullen, 2000).

Institutional research, as an organizational function, can be viewed as a catalyst for fostering a research culture. Historically, institutional research has served as a neutral, data-collecting body that simply created reports to satisfy external mandates (Volkwein, 1999). The traditional role of institutional research has begun to shift to one of catalyst for institutionwide change (Sanford, 1995). In support of the new institutional research role, there has been a call to have the institutional research be more than just a reporting function, and instead to use institutional research in a consultant role for decision making or as a member of a high-level administrative team, thereby bringing a universitywide research perspective to decision making (Johnston and Kristovich, 2000; MacDougall and Friedlander, 1990; Mundhenk, 2000). Such changes in institutional research are seen across the country, specifically at the community college level (Volkwein, 1999).

For example, state-mandated accountability measures are often drafted by legislatures who have little understanding of the implications for the implementation of an institution's access and equity initiatives, much less for the institutional capacity for accurate measurement of these initiatives. Consequently, as in the case of accountability funding for community colleges in California, Oregon, South Carolina, and other states, millions of dollars were given for outcome measures without specifying how the institutions should actually go about meeting those outcomes. It is one matter to award a mathematics enrichment center funds to improve its outreach to low-achieving students; it is another matter to tie that funding to institutional transfer rates. However, do the people who run these programs have evaluation or assessment experience? What steps have they taken to track the effectiveness of their activities? And how will they incorporate the data collection process into their ongoing activities? What kind of access do they have to institutional data? These are the types of questions that the process of creating knowledge-based systems addresses.

These questions are best addressed in a research culture, where funded programs with valuable information about the effectiveness of program practices can then be used to modify those practices to increase the program success and subsequently the success of its students (Wellman, 2001). In other words, the push for accountability drives more meaningful internal change, ultimately leading the institution to apply concepts of organizational learning to its primary goal of student success (Wellman, 2001). A system of self-regulation that ensures high standards across the institution, while at the same time appearing credible to the outside world, is necessary in order to weave together external accountability needs with internal academic structures (Ewell, 1994). Similarly, self-regulation can reduce direct political control, thereby protecting academic freedom (Zumeta, 1998).

A proactive approach to fostering a research culture has been shown to provide a respite from the compliance mentality in higher education (Ewell, 1994). It has also been proposed that institutions need to shift their perspective from one that views accountability as mere bureaucratic reporting to one that foresees a connection between accountability measures and improved teaching and learning, as well as to move beyond state reporting requirements by incorporating research findings that specify areas and procedures for improvement (MacDougall and Friedlander, 1990; Ewell 1991; Wellman, 2001). Subsequently, research cultures are able to confront accountability with a new perspective. Rather than a compliance attitude, a research culture embraces reflection on its practice and strives to implement change. Organizational learning can be sustained by creating a research culture, facilitated by knowledge management and based on internal and external demands, so that ultimately the need for accountability measures and the need to increase capacity to understand and evaluate its programs is met. In this way, the accountability movement is seen as a catalyst to motivate such reflection and knowledge-driven decision making, and external involvement is motivation for institutions to become involved in and appropriately shape the accountability process.

Context and Politics of Information Flow

An examination of the structures and procedures related to the flow of information throughout the organization is perhaps the most neglected aspect in making the shift from data-driven information systems to knowledge-based systems. The reason for this is that if knowledge is understood as information placed in a certain context and therefore embedded with meaning, the flow of information in the organization is likely to be affected by internal structures and procedures related to the creation and dissemination of this information. Context is also composed of the tacit knowledge. Many organizations ease this process of tacit knowledge transfers through the use of storytelling and community-based forums. These forums, which might consist of electronic discussions or postings on an organizational Web site, convey to staff the culture, rituals, and organizational traditions that exist as one component of the history of the organization (Davenport, 1998; Brown, 2000).

Historically, institutional research has been at the center of this information flow by providing interpretation and analysis of data to the organization. However, there are several underlying issues that affect these efforts. These include where the institutional research office is located within the organization in terms of reporting structure, whether it is centralized or decentralized, its decision-making capability, and existing channels of distribution for information. An organization that wishes to create knowledge-based systems will likely face a redesign of internal structures and procedures related to flow of information. However, as is often the case in higher education institutions, the mission of institutional research is not clear and lacks definition, institutional needs are driven by individuals' competing needs, and the end-users of the information are not asked what they need to make better decisions. The institutional researchers themselves have often been left to their own devices to set research priorities and determine who has access to the information. While the rapid sophistication of technology has placed increased demands on institutional research staff, there has also been an increase in the number and complexity of requests for data from institutional research, making the job that much more difficult. Also, there is a growing need to retrain the institutional research staff facing these new challenges (Sanford, 1995).

There are also several political barriers to information sharing. These might include local efforts that duplicate the efforts of institutional research staff due to perceived repercussions of information sharing. For example, in the case of accountability, a department may not want to reveal a breakdown of attrition rates by program within a department if there is a fear of punitive measures (such as the closing of an academic program or the reduction of funding). It may also be that information is tightly controlled within the organization and that the sharing of information is perceived as giving up power. In fact, it is often the case that the sharing of information within an organization has the potential to redistribute decision-making authority and thus impedes the creation of knowledge-based information systems unless they are supported both top-down and bottom-up within the organization (Schein, 1992). Thus, in order to understand how information is produced and transmitted in an organization, it is necessary to study the interactions between those that make up the organization and how they create and disseminate information based on the structure and procedures that support these types of interactions (Petrides, Khanuja-Dhall, and Reguerin, 2000).

Conclusion

In this chapter I have argued that the integration of the institutional research function within the larger context of organizational learning and the creation and maintenance of a research culture facilitated by knowledge management contribute to the success of higher education institutions. The demand for accountability measures and the desire for research that informs decision making help illuminate the demands placed upon institutions to create a research culture that will enable them to meet accountability mandates and increase their capacity to understand and evaluate their academic programs and services. As illustrated above, this process involves an assessment and possible redesign of the internal structures and procedures related to the flow of information throughout an organization, specifically in light of its frontline role in the acquisition and dissemination of information within the organization. Ultimately, the push for accountability can be used to drive more meaningful internal change by increasing an organization's ability to apply concepts of organizational learning to its primary goal of student success.

Although in this chapter I have made the case for the use of organizational learning in the creation of knowledge-based systems, I have also supported the underlying assumption that organizational learning and knowledge-based systems play an important role for institutions of higher education. As Levine states: "An organization that supports information sharing and knowledge creation among its members and is committed to including and reconciling multiple viewpoints is likely to establish effective and efficient processes as well as improve organizational life" (Levine, 2001, p. 23).

Higher education institutions have a growing need for research that can inform decision making. The reconceptualiztion of institutional research as an integrated function of the organization would enable organizations to use comprehensive information for decision making, goal setting, and accountability and integrate organizational needs for common purposes within the institution. These common purposes include identifying information policies, designing new standardized assessment and evaluation procedures, and developing useful and user-friendly information that would allow the institution to make more informed and research-driven policies and procedures and, most important, create knowledge-based systems that support continuous learning in the improvement of programs and services for students and the community.

References

Argyris, C. "Teaching Smart People How to Learn." *Harvard Business Review*, May-June 1991.

Argyris, C., and Schon, D. A. *Organizational Learning II: Theory, Method and Practice.* Reading, Mass.: Addison-Wesley, 1996.

Bernbom, G. "Institution-Wide Information Management and Its Assessment." In R. Katz and J. Rudy (eds.), *Information Technology in Higher Education: Assessing Its Impact and Planning for the Future*, Summer 1999, *102*, 71–83.

Bloodgood, J. M., and Salisbury, W. D. "Understanding the Influence of Organizational Strategies on Information Technology and Knowledge Management Strategies." *Decision Support Systems*, 2001, *31*, 55–69.

Brown, J. S. "Sustaining the Ecology of Knowledge." *Leader to Leader*, Spring 1999, *12*, 31–36.

Brown, J. S. "Growing Up Digital." *Change*, March-April 2000, 11–20.

Brown, J. S., Collins, A., and Duguid, P. "Situated Cognition and the Culture of Learning." *Educational Researcher*, Jan.-Feb. 1989, 32–42.

Cliffe, S. "Knowledge Management: The Well-Connected Business." *Harvard Business Review*, 1998, *76*(4), 17–21.

Coate, L. E. "Beyond Re-engineering: Changing the Organizational Paradigm." In National Association of College and University Business Offices (ed.), *Organizational Paradigm Shifts*. Washington, D.C.: National Association of College and University Business Offices, 1996.

COIL. "Knowledge Ecology." Community Intelligence Labs. [http://www.knowledge ecology.com], 1999.

Davenport, T. H. *Information Ecology: Mastering the Information and Knowledge Environment*. New York: Oxford University Press, 1997.

Davenport, T. H., DeLong, D. W., and Beers, M. C. "Successful Knowledge Management Projects." *Sloan Management Review*, Winter 1998, 43–57.

Davenport, T. H., Eccles, R., and Prusak, L. "Information Politics." *Sloan Management Review*, Fall 1992, 53–65.

Davenport, T. H., and Prusak, L. *Working Knowledge: Managing What Your Organization Knows*. Boston: Harvard Business School Press, 1998.

Drucker, P. "The Coming of the New Organization." *Harvard Business Review*, Jan.-Feb. 1988.

Duffy, J. "Knowledge Management: To Be or Not to Be?" *Information Management Journal*, 2000, *34*(1), 64–67.

Ewell, P. T. "A Matter of Integrity: Accountability and the Future of Self-Regulation." *Change* magazine, 1994, *26*(6), 24–29.

Ewell, P. T. "Back to the Future: Assessment and Public Accountability." *Change*, Nov.-Dec. 1991, 12–17.

Friedman, D., and Hoffman, P. "The Politics of Information." *Change*, May-June 2001, *33*(2), 50–57.

Garvin, D. A., "Building a Learning Organization." *Harvard Business Review*, July-Aug. 1993.

Hansen, M. T., Nohria, N., and Tierney, T. "What's Your Strategy for Managing Knowledge?" *Harvard Business Review*, 1999, *77*(2), 106–116.

Johnson, R. *Setting Our Sights*. Los Angeles: The Achievement Council, 1996.

Johnston, G. H., and Kristovich, S.A.R. "Community College Alchemists: Turning Data into Information." *Dimensions of Managing Academic Affairs in the Community College.* New Directions for Community Colleges, no. 109. San Francisco: Jossey-Bass, 2000.

Laudon, K. C., and Laudon, J. P. *Essentials of Management Information Systems: Organization and Technology in the Networked Enterprise*. Upper Saddle River, N.J.: Prentice Hall, 2001.

Leonard, D., and Straus, S. "Putting Your Company's Whole Brain to Work." *Harvard Business Review,* July-Aug. 1997.

Levine, L. "Integrating Knowledge and Processes in a Learning Organization." *Information Systems Management,* 2001, *18*(1), 21–33.

MacDougall, P. R., and Friedlander, J. "Responding to Mandates for Institutional Effectiveness." *Models for Conducting Institutional Research.* New Directions for Community Colleges, no. 72. San Francisco: Jossey-Bass, 1990.

McDermott, R. "Why Information Technology Inspired But Cannot Deliver Knowledge Management." *California Management Review,* Summer 1999, *41*(4), 103–117.

Mundhenk, R. T. "The Trouble with Outcomes." *Community College Journal,* June-July 2000, *70*(6), 13–15.

Mitchell, M. "Law in Order." *CIO Magazine,* April 1, 2000, 158–162.

Morgan, G. *Images of Organization.* Newbury Park, Calif.: Sage, 1986.

Nettles, M., and Cole, J. "Benchmarking Assessment of Teaching and Learning in Higher Education and Public Accountability: State Governing, Coordinating Board and Regional Accreditation Association Practices and Policies." Stanford, Calif.: National Center for Postsecondary Improvement, 1997.

Peterson, M. W. "The Role of Institutional Research: From Improvement to Redesign." *What Is Institutional Research All About? A Critical and Comprehensive Assessment of the Profession.* New Directions for Institutional Research, no. 104. San Francisco: Jossey Bass, 1999.

Petrides, L., Khanuja-Dhall, S., and Reguerin, P. "The Politics of Information Management." In L. Petrides (ed.), *Case Studies of Information Technology in Higher Education: Implications for Policy and Practice.* Hershey, Penna.: Idea-Group Publishing, 2000.

Petrides, L. "Information-Based Knowledge Systems: The Case for a Knowledge Ecology Perspective in the Community College." Paper presented at RP Group Conference, Lake Arrowhead, Calif., May 2001a.

Petrides, L. "Reporting Mandates vs. Organizational Learning: The Changing Structure and Function of Institutional Research in the Community College." Paper presented at the Association of the Study of Higher Education Conference, Richmond, Va., Nov. 2001b.

Rallis, S. E., and MacMullen, M. M. "Inquiry Minded Schools: Opening Doors for Accountability." *Phi Delta Kappan,* 2000, *81*(10), 766–773.

Sanford, T. R. (ed.) *Preparing for the Information Needs of the Twenty-First Century.* New Directions for Institutional Research, no. 85. San Francisco: Jossey-Bass, 1995.

Schein, E. H. *Organizational Culture and Leadership.* 2nd ed. San Francisco: Jossey-Bass, 1992.

Senge, P. M. *The Fifth Discipline.* New York: Doubleday, 1990.

Senge, P. M. "Communities of Leaders and Learners." *Harvard Business Review,* 1997, *75*(5), 30–32.

Sirotnik, K. A., and Burstein, L. "Making Sense Out of Comprehensive School-Based Information Systems: An Exploratory Investigation." In A. Bank and R. C. Williams (eds.), *Information Systems and School Improvement: Inventing the Future.* New York: Teachers College Press, 1987.

Sveiby, K. E. *The New Organizational Wealth: Managing and Measuring Knowledge Based Assets.* San Francisco: Berrett Koehler, 1997.

Telem, M. "MIS Implementation in Schools: A Systems Socio-Technical Framework." *Computers in Education,* Jan. 1996, *27*(2), 85–93.

Volkwein, F. J. "The Four Faces of Institutional Research." *What Is Institutional Research All About? A Critical and Comprehensive Assessment of the Profession.* New Directions for Institutional Research, no. 104. San Francisco: Jossey-Bass, 1999.

Walleri, R. D., and Stoering, J. M. "The Assessment Matrix: Communicating Assessment and Accountability Requirements to the Campus Community." *Journal of Applied Research in the Community College,* 1996, *4*(1), 23–38.

Wellman, J. V. "Assessing State Accountability Systems." *Change,* March-April 2001, *33*(2), 47–52.

Wells, J., Silk, E., and Torres, D. "Accountability, Technology, and External Access to Information: Implications for IR." *How Technology Is Changing Institutional Research.* New Directions for Institutional Research, no 103. San Francisco: Jossey-Bass, 1999.

Wenger, E. C., and Snyder, W. M. "Communities of Practice: The Organizational Frontier." *Harvard Business Review,* 2000, *78*(1), 139–145.

Zisman, M. "Start Talking and Get to Work." Paper presented at the KM World Conference, Dallas, Texas, Sept. 23, 1999.

Zumeta, W. "Accountability: Challenges for Higher Education." *Policy Studies Review,* 1998, *15*(4), 5–22.

LISA A. PETRIDES *is a professor in the department of organization and leadership at Columbia University, Teachers College in New York.*

6

Many technologies and products can be used to support knowledge management. Based on the purposes they serve, they can be classified in one or more of the following categories: business intelligence, collaboration, content and document management, e-learning, knowledge base, portals, customer relationship management, data mining, workflow, and search. The authors propose a model focused on technologies and products likely to be used most frequently by institutional researchers.

Technologies, Products, and Models Supporting Knowledge Management

Jing Luan, Andreea M. Serban

"Knowledge management is the Holy Grail of the modern company, much rumored but rarely found. Many software solutions—from document management and data mining to search engines and portals—have claimed to be the key, only to fail. 'Knowledge management is a mix of all those disciplines with a good dose of know-how on top,' opines Elise Olding, vice president for knowledge, e-learning and collaboration at the Hurwitz Group, a Framingham, Massachusetts-based consultancy. In other words, knowledge management can't be found in a shrink-wrapped box" (Prewitt, 2001). Indeed, as discussed in previous chapters, technology by itself will be insufficient to create and sustain knowledge management; however, it is highly unlikely, if not impossible, to implement a knowledge management infrastructure without the support of technology. Such an infrastructure needs to be comprehensive enough to facilitate the knowledge management processes discussed in Chapter One ranging from capturing to sharing of knowledge. As such, no single product or technology is sufficient but some are necessary as building blocks.

Technology Taxonomy and Supporting Products

The technologies supporting knowledge management have evolved around the processes described in the opening chapter. They can be grouped in one or more of the following categories:

- Business intelligence
- Knowledge base
- Collaboration

- Content and document management
- Portals
- Customer relationship management
- Data mining
- Workflow
- Search
- E-learning

Some of these categories were discussed in detail in prior chapters. In the following section they will be defined and examples of supporting products will be provided. The products listed by no means cover all options available, nor are they meant to be prescriptive. They are intended to inform readers about some of the products currently available and their functionality and capabilities. Given the fast advance of technologies in this field, by the time this volume is published, other, more powerful and sophisticated products or refinements of the ones presented in this chapter will probably become available.

Choosing to implement one or more products supporting knowledge management depends on many factors, including

- Scope and breath of the knowledge management strategy sought
- Time frame for implementation
- Implementation strategy (for example, comprehensive or targeted on specific organizational units and functions)
- Financial and human resources available
- Need to continue to use applications already in place

The categories discussed and products presented as examples are not necessarily discrete. That is, there is some degree of overlap between some of these categories and the functionality of the products that support them. Some products can support two or more of these categories.

Business Intelligence

Systematic gathering and accessing of intelligence, knowledge, about competitors is one of the main interests of organizations, whether businesses or higher education. Activities such as environmental scanning and benchmarking are just two examples of such interests that many higher education institutions undertake on a periodic basis. Such activities would be greatly facilitated if organizations could create some form of an electronic reference library that would be constantly updated as new relevant information becomes available. Business intelligence applications, such as Vigil's e-Sense, "map complex business landscapes without the assistance of the IT department. These maps contain listings of companies, kinds of information sought, and specific questions relating to that information. Once the maps are created, the system can monitor both public and private networks for relevant information in real time" (Wallach, 2000).

Business intelligence applications are also used to gather and organize data and information existing in internal sources. Some of these applications, such as MicroStrategy's Transactor, can "collect data from back-end databases, Web servers, and enterprise resource planning (ERP) systems, according to predefined criteria. It then pushes that information out as actionable content in eXtended Markup Language (XML) format, so a desktop computer with a Web browser, a personal digital assistant, and even a telephone enabled with the Wireless Application Protocol (WAP) subset of XML can receive it. A user who has received this information can send back an action request to Transactor, which in turn prompts a back-end system to complete a transaction" (Gill, 2000). Several examples of business intelligence products are summarized in Table 6.1.

Knowledge Base

Closely linked to business intelligence, knowledge base refers to databases and repositories of data, information, and knowledge. The primary purpose of knowledge base applications is to create such repositories in a structured fashion that can facilitate searching and circulating knowledge throughout the organization. Table 6.2 lists several examples of such applications.

Collaboration

One of the core tenets of knowledge management is the ability to collaborate, including collaboration among employees within an organization, collaboration between different organizations, and even collaboration between different computer systems without human interaction. The latter aspect of collaboration is known as peer-to-peer computing (P2P). Examples of P2P include schema for distributing latest antivirus updates and software patches such as the one supported by the Network Associates Inc.'s business security site MyCIO.com or P2P working groups such as the one started by Intel Corp., joined with Hewlett-Packard Co., IBM Corp., and other players, whose goal is to foster common standards and protocols for P2P in business environments (Barth, 2001).

More important, however, is the emphasis on human interaction through virtual spaces and means. Such collaboration, whether Web based or using messaging or file sharing, needs to occur without the information technology (IT) department's intervention every time collaboration is needed. The pioneer of collaboration applications has been Lotus with its application Lotus Notes launched in 1998. Since then many products have been developed that provide users with the ability to work collaboratively,

Table 6.1. Business Intelligence Products

Product	Description	Vendor
Esense	Based on predefined criteria, it collects and updates on real-time information residing on internal and external Web servers, creating a virtual reference library.	Vigil Technologies [www.esense.com]
Transactor	Collects data from internal and external sources such as back-end databases, Web servers, and transactional systems based on predefined criteria and pushes the resulting information to a user, who in turn can send a request for action to the application. The software prompts a back-end system to complete the transaction.	MicroStrategy [www.microstrategy.com]
Genio Suite	Integrated data platform that transforms, cleanses, enriches and directs information across the entire spectrum of decision support systems, data warehouses, data marts, and enterprise applications such as enterprise resource planning (ERP), customer relationship management (CRM), and financial systems. Features include a time- and event-based scheduler and a tool for designing customized views of metadata. Genio is compatible with various database management systems.	Hummingbird Ltd. [www.hummingbird.com]
Noetix Enterprise Technology Suite	Integrated set of products designed to simplify and accelerate reporting throughout the organization. A stand-alone suite for Oracle applications, it automatically detects and adapts to an organization's application configurations to enable users to make specific queries. The suite includes NoetixViews, Noetix Query Server, Noetix Web Query, and AnswerPoint.	Noetix Corp. [www.noetix.com]
SPSS WebApp Framework	This software development kit for Web-based analytical applications allows users to build customized programs for predictive analysis such as purchasing trends, survey results processing and sales forecasts. It provides automated reports in a variety of formats.	SPSS Inc. [www.spss.com]
WebFocus 4.3.6	This program enables sorting, filtering, reporting on, and graphing internal and external data in a range of databases and systems. It distributes custom-designed reports internally and externally and automatically reformats them for wireless devices. Users can also reconfigure reports and graphs into Web pages for remote viewing.	Information Builders [www.informationbuilders.com]

Table 6.2. Knowledge Base Products

Product	Description	Vendor
QKS Classifier	This taxonomy platform organizes content into a directory that gives users control over categorization decisions. The XML-based system integrates into existing Intranets, Extranets, portals, and corporate Web sites.	Quiver Inc. [www.quiver.com]
Thoughtscape Suite	Suite of personal e-research comprising components. Any of the following five components can be configured and customized to fit corporate branding. Thoughtscape DE—(Desktop Edition) helps personalize research by adding Web pages, attached files, notes, and e-mail to communicate perspective. Thoughtscape WE—(Web Edition) allows users to navigate and edit concept-clustered search results. Thoughtscape RE—(Report Engine) facilitates sharing knowledge and findings in a variety of presentation formats to accelerate decision making. Thoughtscape NE—(Notification Engine) creates alerts that automatically monitor key content for changes. Thoughtscape KL—(Knowledge Library) enhances project collaboration with a Web-based knowledge library.	ThoughtShare Communications Inc. [www.thoughtshare.com]
Noetix Enterprise Technology Suite (NETS)	Integrated solution that allows organizations to simplify access to data, translate data into familiar business terms, and deliver information over the wired and wireless Internet. It maps data locations and generates metadata to systematically design, create, and populate a data warehouse. Users can then search, view, and retrieve warehoused data. Automatic upgrade protection prevents data loss when the warehouse is updated.	Noetix Corp. [www.noetix.com]
QueryObject System	This Java-based tool allows users to build, organize, and query knowledge bases through the Internet or a company's Intranet. Most third-party search tools can access the knowledge bases it creates. QueryObject is compatible with multiple systems and data forms, including XML.	QueryObject Systems Corp. [www.queryobject.com]
Tacit KnowledgeMail and ESP	Both products manage text-based search among non-coded knowledge base. ESP has a developer's toolkit.	Tacit Systems [www.tacit.com]

any time, regardless of physical location. Table 6.3 lists several examples of such applications.

Content and Document Management

The ability to manage documents and content over the Web has been recognized as key to a sound knowledge management infrastructure. As Wallach (2001) describes: "It's a common metaphor in business that everyone involved in a project should be on the same page. Yet many enterprises

Table 6.3. Collaboration Products

Product	Description	Vendor
AskMe Enterprise 5.3	Along with reporting capabilities, this system stores all information transferred in a searchable knowledge base, which can also include FAQs, resources, files, and links, all of which are organized by topic. AE enables employees to identify coworkers who can solve specific business problems and answer day-to-day questions. Each employee can have a customizable, searchable profile containing information about his or her professional background and areas of expertise, as well as links to past answers, FAQs, and more. As employees use the system, the answers they provide become part of their searchable profiles. Profiles can be categorized in an organized taxonomy that mirrors a company's business issues. The profiles are accessible via e-mail, Intranets, and search engines.	AskMe Corp. [www.askme.com]
Domino 2.0/Lotus NotesR5	Domino provides integrated application services that optimize the platform for rapid delivery of the collaborative Web applications. Built-in connection services provide live access to relational databases and ERP applications. Lotus NotesR5 is known for its groupware capabilities.	IBM [www.ibm.com]
eRoom 5.4	Provides a digital workplace, allowing organizations to assemble a project team wherever people are located and manage the collaborative activities that support their complex and rapidly changing projects and processes.	eRoom Technology. Inc. [www.eroom.com]
HotComm 1.0	Working with IM-Live and ezPeer, this desktop client-based collaboration tool networks with other peers to allow multiple sessions and interactive communications in a secured mode.	1stWorks Corp. [www.hotcomm.com]
Infocetera Information Management System 1.0	Targeted for users in medium-sized companies that need a suite of information management and group collaboration tools. It is directory tree based software that incorporates features such as instant messaging, access control, search, discussion board, and calendaring.	WTS Systems LLC [www.infocetera.com]
KnowledgeLEAD™	Functions as a tool on the Intranet to identify skills, work experiences, and expertise of the company employees. The system enables knowledge sharing and collaboration among employees.	Cadenza Inc. [www.KnowledgeLEAD.com]
Simplify 2.1	Targeted for Communities of Practice, it provides a solution to online interactive Web environment. Its main feature is the Yahoo-Google style treatment to information context. Users have control over style and customization.	Tomoye [www.tomoye.com]
WebSpace	It is able to link dispersed teams of individuals or groups in a virtual and centralized Web environment to share documents, hold discussions, and conduct project tasks. Services require a separate host.	Copernus Inc. [www.copernus.com]

Table 6.4. Content and Document Management Products

Product	Description	Vendor
Astoria	Application for managing technical and structured document automation and publication. Works with all types of contents for technical publications, including graphs, SGML, and XML.	Chrystal Software Inc. [www.chrystal.com]
LiquidOffice, TELEform	Working jointly, TELEform converts paper data into online database driven information. LiquidOffice provides services for managing virtual form submitting, routing, and verifying. LiquidOffice uses XML, HTML, and Adobe PDF standards.	Cardiff Software Inc. [www.cardiff.com]
Rhythmyx Content Manager 4.0	It uses an XML-based platform coupled with open standards for future expansion. It automates content creation, approval, and publication to Web sites and incorporates content management.	Percussion Software Inc. [www.percussion.com]
Teamsite Suite	Working in sync with a suite of software, it deals with comprehensive aspects of creating, managing, publishing, and maintaining content.	Interwoven [www.interwoven.com]
TMS Products	Three products aimed at different levels of usage. TMSWeb provides training and document management services for large companies. Services include publishing knowledge-based documents and review and approval capabilities using Adobe electronic signatures. It is based on Windows platform.	Quality Systems Integrators Inc. [www.qsi-inc.com]
Vignette Content Suite	Comprehensive, integrated, and technologically neutral platform for creating, managing, and publishing content as well as e-commerce.	Vignette [www.vignette.com]

find themselves in a situation where mission-critical documents and other forms of corporate content get shoveled onto their intranet or extranet without efficient management of versions, ownership, or timeliness of the material." Duplication of documents and inability to determine quickly which version is the official one are aspects with which we all have had to contend at some point. Table 6.4 includes several examples of such applications.

Portals

In 1999, Roberts-Witt stated, "Knowledge management has found its killer app. The enterprise information portal—simple in concept but previously elusive in practice—is suddenly front and center on the IT agenda. Bringing together in one embodiment the notions of business intelligence, document classification, text analysis, group collaboration, executive information, and the company intranet, it promises to provide what we've been looking for from computers since the days of Norbert Wiener and Vannevar Bush." Indeed, as discussed in more detail in Chapter Three, portals have garnered tremendous popularity in the business world and have made headway in higher education as well. What they appeared to promise in 1999 they have generally delivered to those organizations that decided to implement them.

Some higher education institutions, seeing the potential of this technology, have joined forces and created the only currently free portal for higher education, the uPortal created by the JA-SIG group with support from the Andrew W. Mellon Foundation. At the time of the writing, six campuses have this portal in production ("live" sites):

California Polytechnic State University	[http://my.calpoly.edu/]
Denison University	[http://my.denison.edu/]
Laurentian University	[http://portal.laurentian.ca/render.uP]
University of British Columbia	[http://www.itservices.ubc.ca/myubc/]
University of California, Irvine	[http://snap.uci.edu/]

Twelve other major universities, including Princeton, Columbia, and Yale, are running demos. There are many portal applications available and some of them are listed in Table 6.5.

Customer Relationship Management

The purposes and functionality of CRM have been discussed in detail in Chapter Four. Table 6.6 includes some examples of CRM products currently available.

Data Mining

As discussed in Chapter Three, data mining is one of the knowledge management techniques that has direct applicability to the work of institutional researchers. Data mining applications vary from client versions that can be installed on a PC and used by a single user at a time, such as SPSS's Clementine 7.0, to hosted applications that combine business intelligence, knowledge base, and data mining capabilities such as DigiMine Analytic Services. Table 6.7 summarizes several data mining applications.

Workflow

Gaining effectiveness and efficiency in all operational aspects of an organization has been a continuous quest ever since the beginning of the industrial revolution. The knowledge management framework acknowledges that competitiveness can be enhanced through better ways of automating as many of the routine operational processes as possible as well as emphasizing the need for creating an infrastructure that integrates operations.

Table 6.5. Portal Products

Product	Description	Vendor
Citrix Nfuse	Citrix Systems provides both server and portal products. NFuse, the portal software, integrates other applications, such as Windows, UNIX, and Java, into the portal environment, which results in an individualized interface. Users are able to access the portal via a secured and single access point.	Citrix Systems, Inc. [www.citrix.com]
Oracle iPortal	Described in Chapter 3.	Oracle [www.oracle.com]
Plumtree Corporate Portal	It provides uniformity in access and allows customization. Through a uniform interface, users have access to all data to which they are granted access. It includes multiple search engines and content management components. It has wireless data access capacity as well.	Plumtree [www.plumtree.com]
uPortal	Free to higher education institutions and developed jointly by members of JA-SIG, uPortal can stand alone or co-exist with the overall organizational Web structure. Customized features incorporate discussion forums, chat, and on-line data collection and surveys. uPortal is an open-standard effort using Java, XML, JSP, and J2EE.	JA-SIG [www.ja-sig.org]
Yahoo PortalBuilder	Java-based server software. Features include content management, ability to integrate e-mail, databases, and corporate management in a single interface and access point.	Corporate Yahoo [www.corporate.yahoo.com]

Workflow applications cover a wide array of operational processes from routine ones such as form routing (CaseFlow) to complex, integrated organizational activities such as data-gathering, scenario testing, and trends assessment (Blue Pumpkin Director Enterprise 3.0). Table 6.8 summarizes several examples of such applications.

Search Products

As discussed in prior chapters, the amount of data and information available in organizations has increased exponentially. One of the major challenges is to find the appropriate information and obtain it in a format that is user friendly and easy to share. To make matters even more complicated, it is often the case that one has only a vague idea about what exactly one is looking for; that is, if we knew exactly what we needed (for example, the name of a document) and where it is stored, we would not need search capabilities. In recent years, sophisticated search applications have been developed that can create taxonomies based on pattern recognition (for example, the type of key words or phrases used) and can access information stored across

Table 6.6. CRM Products

Product	Description	Vendor
E.piphany	Incorporates analytical and operational CRM and unifies both inbound and outbound customer data in real time. It is designed for Web-based applications.	E.piphany [www.epiphany.com]
eRelationship Suite	eRelationship is the back-end of the entire suite of CRM solutions from Pivotal. It works together with the eRelationship suite of sales, marketing, and service to provide a comprehensive CRM platform that tracks, captures, and consolidates all customer data. Other capabilities include calendaring, Action Objects, and Contact Management.	Pivotal [www.pivotal.com]
PeopleSoft CRM	Entirely Web-based, this software merges major enterprise activities, financials, sales, customer tracking, and marketing on one platform. Its analytical function monitors trends, profitability, and customer channels.	PeopleSoft [www.peoplesoft.com]
Siebel eBusiness Applications	Siebel eBusiness Applications enable organizations to create a single source of customer information, which facilitates selling to, marketing to, and servicing customers across multiple channels, including the Web, call centers, field, resellers, retail, and dealer networks.	Siebel [www.siebel.com]
TIME	Talisma Interaction Management Engine (TIME) is the backbone of the Talisma CRM Suite, integrating business applications, customer profiles, work processes, and communication channels. It utilizes a universal queuing and routing engine that interacts with communication channels of phone, e-mail, online forms, discussion, and in-person.	Talisma [www.talisma.com]

multiple servers and in various repositories and formats. Examples are listed in Table 6.9.

E-Learning

Many organizations have come to recognize that ongoing training for their workforce is the only way to maintain competitiveness in changing environments. Knowledge workers must be able to adapt and acquire new skills as technologies and domains evolve. However, organizations are also sensitive to issues related to time and costs involved in training employees. E-learning has emerged as a viable solution that deals with the need for continuous, on-demand training that is less expensive than the traditional in-classroom format, which takes away employees days at a time. There are many products supporting e-learning and Table 6.10 captures a few examples.

Table 6.7. Data Mining Products

Product	Description	Vendor
Clementine	Has a comprehensive suite of modeling algorithms and can work with a variety of data sources. It utilizes CRISP-DM principles to accomplish knowledge discovery in databases. It provides automatic tipping on what algorithms are possible based on the data.	SPSS, Inc. [Spss.com/Clementine/]
Darwin	Oracle has embedded data mining within its database product Oracle 9i, with all model-building and scoring functions available through a Java-based API.	Oracle [www.oracle.com/ip/analyze/warehouse/datamining/]
Digital Excavator	With strong emphasis on data setup, Digital Excavator uses its X-SET™ technology. It iteratively explores the data, integrates disparate data sources, and massages data into model-ready sets. It enables the application to access multiple data sets directly instead of relying on the structure-based approach used by relational databases.	Digital Archaeology [www.digarch.com]
DigiMine Solutions	With five stand-alone products, DigiMine provides analytical services in enterprise level analytics, as well as eBusiness and campaign response analytics. With interactive reporting, the Enterprise Analytics provides unit, departmental data mining. eBusiness Analytics concentrates on customer behaviors and product sales analysis.	DigiMine Inc. [www.digimine.com]
Enterprise Miner	Addresses the entire data mining process through a point-and-click graphical user interface (GUI). Combined with SAS data warehousing and OLAP technologies, it creates an end-to-end solution.	SAS [www.sas.com/products/miner/]

Tiered Knowledge Management Model (TKMM)

The categories and products discussed so far in this chapter represent a broad array of knowledge management supporting technologies. This discussion has not yet addressed how traditional applications used by institutional researchers, such as reporting and data querying tools, fit into a knowledge management framework. Based on extensive research and actual experience, we propose a tiered knowledge management model (TKMM) for managing knowledge from an institutional research perspective (Figure 6.1). As with any model, it is assumed that the model itself will remain robust and stable, while the specific techniques and technologies may change over time, as they should.

Figure 6.1 shows that knowledge management is a hierarchical process that relies on building blocks (Tier One) and information (Tier Two) to reach the highest form of "knowing" (Tiers Two and Three). These two tiers

Table 6.8. Workflow Products

Product	Description	Vendor
Blue Pumpkin Director— Enterprise	Based on the action framework of Plan, Execute, and Evaluate, it focuses on resolving customer contact related business objectives and work processes. Features include forecasting and scheduling; agent interaction; workforce planning; data-collection; scenario testing; online self-service knowledge base access; and automated management tools for human resources and performance assessment.	Blue Pumpkin Software Inc. [www.blue-pumpkin.com]
CaseFlow	Brings together disparate work processes through entry document processing modules, streamlined work processes, user-defined business rules, and communication generation functions. CaseFlow can cover a large portion of the common workflow functions required in various business process automation systems, including the public sector.	American Management Systems [www.ams.com]
ViewStar, Government Solutions	One of the five products by eiStream, Government Solutions focuses on improving work process automation for public agencies. Coupled with the ViewStar system, work flow issues are resolved in a networked environment in which digital media, data capturing, document generation and other everyday business processes are managed by workflow applications.	eiStream, Inc. [www.eistream.com]

act upon information that translates into the most valuable assets, wisdom, insights, or expertise of an organization.

Model Explained. The flow-chart in Figure 6.2 attempts to capture the process of knowledge management by providing a few examples to illustrate each tier.

Explicit Knowledge. Tier One of explicit knowledge contains granular data. In the examples given in Figure 6.2, student enrollment data typically include demographics, course enrollment, and even financial aid. Learning outcome data may include, for example, grades and institution(s) the student transferred to or from. Census data contain household income and other demographic information by census tracks, zip codes, or county.

In this example, data in Tier One flow to a higher tier where unitary data are aggregated or charted to show the enrollment trend over multiple semesters. Learning outcome data are calculated for GPA and success and retention rates by course, department, or college. The same type of treatment to census data results in information detailing educational levels, income levels, and other pertinent statistics useful for determining a variety of management and curriculum decisions. The activities to obtain the above information are labeled as information processing, which allows slice-and-dice of aggregate statistics. This information processing represents a fair

Table 6.9. Search Products

Product	Description	Vendor
AMI Enterprise Discovery, AMI Website Access	Enterprise Discovery is for Intranet document search and Website Access is for Extranet site management. Both use sophisticated query technology to organize search results and tackle the common search problems of "no-match" or "numerous irrelevant matches." Other features are plain language query capability, multilanguage error tolerance, and automated personalization results presentation.	Go Albert, Inc. [www.albert.com]
BASIS®	Web-based software designed for document collection and search and retrieval. It features records management, document publishing, archiving, product catalog management, and competitive intelligence analysis.	Open Text Corporation [www.opentext.com]
RecomMind	Powered by Probabilistic Latent Semantic Indexing (PLSI) algorithm and XML, this platform-independent solution focuses on turning information overload into information assets. RecomMind features three main areas: intelligent information retrieval, automated categorization, and e-mail-text-data sharing.	RecomMind Inc. [www.recommind.com]
VewDirect	ViewDirect provides scalable high-speed indexed access and electronic distribution of organizational information. ViewDirect suite provides Extranet-Intranet access to documents, integrates back-office systems, and works with a variety of media.	Mobius Management Systems Inc. [www.mobius.com]

share of the type of an institutional researcher's duties. The actual manner in which reporting is done may vary, such as Web-based distribution or other variations of approaches to massaging data. As useful as it may be, such reporting has two limitations. It can severely limit the insights into the vast hidden patterns in data, and it quickly becomes unmanageable when a given table needs to contain three or more dimensions of data; for example, student enrollment by age by term and by gender. The threshold for stepping into more sophisticated knowledge seeking is data mining as discussed in Chapter Two. Only data mining algorithms can answer predicative questions related to, say, student persistence, such as which individual student is likely to persist. For GPA, the algorithms will identify clusters of students, and their ranges of GPA will give insights to how best to teach or assess them. For census data, the algorithms can also provide rule-based reasoning that lists nonacademic factors associated with certain course taking patterns, which in turn affects what to offer and where to offer the classes.

Tacit Knowledge. Managing tacit knowledge requires the availability of a knowledge base (Tier One). Knowledge management is first of all human concentric, meaning that without knowledgeable human intervention there would not be any explicit knowledge, and if there were, it would

Table 6.10. E-Learning Products

Product	Description	Vendor
eLearning Suite	Mainly developed for training sales workers, the eLearning suite, consisting of eTraining and Siebel Distance Learning, provides automated content management, methods of measuring learning, and course content delivery. These two applications can be purchased and deployed together or as stand-alone products.	Siebel [www.siebel.com]
e-Learning System	Targeted for large and mid-sized organizations, this learning management system enables users to develop, launch, and track Web-based training systems and sites. The entire system is hosted off-site to reduce in-house resources. Existing course materials can also be converted for on-line learning.	GeoLearning Inc. [www.geolearning.com]
Human Capital Management Suite	The suite includes trademark KP Performance, KP Learning, and KP Content. Learners can create customized blended on-line learning curricula. Products test and track learner progress and activities.	KnowledgePlanet Inc. [www.knowledgeplanet.com]
TrainNet	Consisting of five modules, this virtual and integrated on-line learning system works for a variety of delivery modalities. It integrates full-screen video with live interaction, using audio conferencing, synchronized Web content, application sharing, embedded e-mail, and whiteboard and Q&A features.	Mentergy Inc. [www.mentergy.com]
Vuepoint Learning System 3.0	Four modules make up this e-learning and content management system: a Web-based evaluation, teaching, and research tool; a student testing and course tracking program; a template-based content creator; and an off-line viewer for asynchronous learning. Such an integrated system allows a company to save multiple authoring and licensing fees and to conduct real-time course management.	Vuepoint Corp. [www.vuepoint.com]

Figure 6.1. Tiered Knowledge Management Model (TKMM)

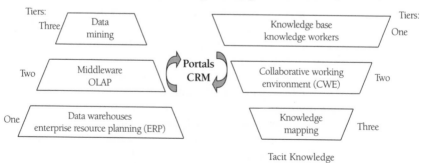

Figure 6.2. Illustration of TKMM

Explicit Knowledge

Tier One	Tier Two	Tier Three
Data Holding Medium	**Information Processing**	**Data Mining**
Student enrollment data →	Enrollment trends analysis →	Which student is likely to persist?
Learning outcome data →	Student GPA report →	Which clusters of students will have GPA>3.75?
Census data →	Socio-economic status →	What are associated with any course-taking pattern?

Portals
CRM

Decisions
Insights
Knowledge
Competencies
Accountability

Tacit Knowledge

Tier One	Tier Two	Tier Three
Knowledge Base	**Collaborative Working Environment**	**Knowledge Mapping**
Personal experiences	Organization structures	Faculty Experts
Skills	Curricula	Group Leaders
Values	Mission statements/Policies	Librarians
Relationships	Manuals	Analysts/Institutional Researchers

stay meaningless. There are far more contextual, noncodified, and unstructured data existing within an employee's mind (knowledge worker) than those listed in the flow chart. As discussed in Chapter One, what is possessed by knowledge workers is mostly unstructured and hard to codify and yet most crucial and instrumental to an organization's operation and survival. Therefore, the organization needs to bring the knowledge out of the minds of knowledge workers through knowledge sharing. Tier Two exemplifies such processes. The arrows pointing to items in Tier Two refer to the influence each kind of tacit knowledge (personal experiences, skills, values, and so on) can have on Tier Two. Arrows with thicker lines denote more direct influence. Such an environment is a collaborative work environment (CWE). As discussed earlier, a number of technologies and techniques are available for use in CWE in managing Tier Two of tacit knowledge. Consulting firms have been pioneers in managing tacit knowledge. To the extent they can, they use groupware to make published reports available to everyone on the Intranet. If the person is outside the firewall, VPN (Virtual Private Network) tunnels will be established for knowledge sharing. E-mails are culled and stored to help compensate for the lack of time for detailed documentation and report writing.

In Tier Three of tacit knowledge, the organization conducts *knowledge mapping,* a term coined by Davenport and Prusak (1998). In principle, knowledge management is about locating knowledge sources; it is not about knowing everything, but knowing or finding where everything is. The past century has seen information and knowledge accumulated exponentially—more than all the previous millennia combined. Through time, however, our biological brain has not changed much; therefore, remembering every piece of information is impossible. What is possible, in knowledge management, is to create a different kind of organizational chart. This chart, or knowledge map, contains no ranks, but the skills and experiences of every employee.

Finally, linked by a portal, explicit knowledge and tacit knowledge work together. As discussed in Chapter One, these two types of knowledge interact and, at times, intertwine. In TKMM, their interactions occur at Tiers Two and Three. Thanks to modern technology, the ways in which they interact have become more pervasive and ever more available. Portal technologies have allowed knowledge workers to access explicit data and information with a few keystrokes. Enterprise knowledge portals are powerful in managing both data and text-based knowledge (Mitchell, 2001; Moskowitz, 2001). A number of vendors are showcasing products that can scan e-mail messages to store and categorize the vast amount of tacit information and knowledge that employees produce in their e-mail. Case Based Reasoning is the technology that extracts knowledge from narrative forms, such as case studies, documents, and other problem domains. Modern library science, coupled with search engines, has made the portal a place where competitive intelligence and vast amounts of product or research literature is available.

Back to explicit knowledge, TKMM comprises three tiers: data holding medium, information processing, and data mining. We use a few examples below to further describe the application of the model. Knowledge management in the institutional research setting is primarily the management of explicit knowledge with a small amount of tacit knowledge. Tacit knowledge may be converted into explicit knowledge, such as data from surveys where information is cut and diced into categories and ranks. Not all tacit data or information can or needs to become explicit knowledge. Schreiber, Akkermans, and Anjewierden (2000) established the technical base for codifying tacit knowledge down to the code (programming) level. Their techniques still remain to be applied in real life.

Data warehousing, data querying and reporting, and data mining technologies have greatly enhanced the status of explicit knowledge. The following topography provides a delineation of the layers of these technologies and required skills.

Enterprise Resource Planning (ERP) systems in Tier One, such as Peoplesoft, Oracle, Datatel, or SAP, are primarily the source for most of the data that researchers need, short of surveys and other supplemental sources. These systems are on-line transaction processing (OLTP) applications that maintain the most scattered and fragmented relational data files, for good reason. OLTP data should first be prepared using extract, transformation, and load techniques that include staging and denormalizing to move into a data warehouse on a database server, such as SQL Server.

Figure 6.3. Topography of Tiered Knowledge Management Model (TKMM) for Explicit Knowledge

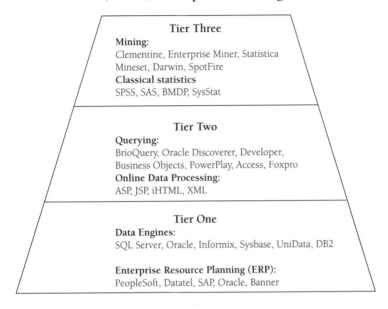

Note: this topography for TKMM is for illustrative purposes only. Not all products by all vendors are displayed, nor are any products shown necessarily endorsed.

There are basically two types of tools in Tier Two. One is for querying data and the other is for on-line data collection and display. Many of the query tools have Web functions, such as BrioInsight and Oracle Discoverer, which can access data over the Web and display the results to the Web. Greater emphasis is already starting to be placed on Web-based processes that will shape research, planning, and all types of activities that are currently done off-line. Web technology has spun off software programs to have its own data collection, querying, and displaying capacities. For example, using ASP (active server pages), users can overlay scripts on top of SQL or Access to produce dynamic html pages. Various online surveys first use the software to display a form; it then collects the data and stores them in a database. As discussed in Chapter Three, portal technologies have made possible developing and deploying Web-based querying and displaying without the need for ASP. However, for those institutions that are not ready to implement portals, ASP remains a viable solution. Access and FoxPro are considered to be desktop database programs. They are used for relational database querying. Tier Two uses programs that require middleware to act as a go-between of servers (data holding medium) and clients (desktop computer with software programs) for data querying and reporting. Based on the nature of the data and the needs of reporting, querying software may be directly installed on the server for faster processing. This is called the "thin client" model. The less processing done on the client side, the "thinner" the client becomes.

As data warehouses grow in size and complexity, and the level of sophistication and appetite of decision makers and knowledge workers increase, traditional techniques for data analysis simply cannot satisfy the knowledge sought from the data and information. Artificial intelligence (AI) and neural networks that excel in working with enormously "thick" data files have matured and evolved into data mining. We have housed data mining in the Tier Three. The more recent trends in data mining, data visualization, and real-time customer service produce more challenges in skills update and require more tech savvy in working with data warehouses.

Tier Three of this model also points to traditional (classical) statistical packages, as well as data mining software programs. Just to demonstrate that the three tiers are not necessarily always hierarchical, a number of database engines now host data mining algorithms as well. This trend has several benefits. It reduces the amount of data validation and standardization time, now that the data and the algorithms are in one place. When a field in the database changes, it changes the corresponding field in the algorithm. Another benefit is timeliness. Patterns are immediately uncovered from the real-time data or time-delayed data.

Four challenges continue to exist. They are data warehousing technologies, Web-based data access, real-time querying and reporting capabilities, and data mining. Data warehousing is a matured industry; however, implementation of data warehouses in higher education is not. A large number of institutions, realizing its necessity, are scrambling to build data warehouses from the ground up by dipping into the ERP applications' on-line transactional databases. Different data warehouse designs have emerged. Some use the Star Schema, and others rely primarily on data marts. Emphasis is shifting toward maintaining metadata (data about data) or electronic DED (data element dictionary) in order to assure data integrity and consistency.

With the advent of sophisticated querying capabilities, the field is demanding real-time querying, which means the data warehouse needs to be refreshed on a daily, hourly, or even minute-by-minute basis, requiring strong commitment for support in network and storage from IT departments. Purely Internet-based enterprises may not sustain the market forces, but enterprises cannot survive without moving toward the Web. In any type of large-scale project designs, it is common practice to first consider Web based—so much so that data warehouses must be brought out of the vault and over the firewall. Querying tool vendors have quickly adapted their products for this purpose as well. In the past decade, as cadres of researchers have acquired skills in working with querying tools to produce decision support reports as the middleware, data querying and report industries have matured. Some have been very successful in working with multidimensional data cubes to produce reports. This trend needs to continue.

Significance of TKMM

TKMM has significant implications for researchers in the areas of securing funding, updating knowledge, managing the office, outsourcing, and understanding the relationships between research and other technology-intensive departments on campuses. Specifically, such a model may guide institutional research in the following areas:

- Project management. This model explains what tool is appropriate for which project. For example, for real-time query as in minute-by-minute enrollment reporting, one would most likely use OLAP tools; for producing reports (on-line or off-line), one would most likely use relational database querying tools.
- Skills update. This model describes the relationship of the software programs in each tier and the level of knowledge needed for each. For example, to be comfortable with what is in Tier Two, one should be familiar with Javascripts, ASP, and SQL (Structured Query Language) and many others.
- Managing the office. The model helps institutional researchers identify on which tier they have strength and for which tier they need to work with other departments. It helps them determine standard operating procedures; for example, understanding how data are processed into data warehouses and by whom and what institutional researchers should expect from their IT departments.
- Resource planning. This model guides the planning and allocation of resources for research. For example, institutional researchers can successfully argue why and in what software and hardware to invest and when to upgrade.
- Outsourcing. Not all institutional research offices are equipped fully with expertise and staff to perform all tasks in all three tiers. The traditional competencies of institutional are in Tier Three and the report design and analysis tasks in Tier Two. These tasks are better managed in-house. Other tasks, especially those that are more IT extensive, may be candidates for outsourcing.
- Promoting and advocating for institutional research. With this model, institutional researchers can clearly converse with professionals in adjacent fields, such as marketing, auditing, and testing. The classification of tools and the delineation of boundaries among the tasks in each tier also help institutional researchers articulate their needs to decision makers and IT offices.

References

Barth, S. "The Promise of Peerless Platforms: Is Peer-to-Peer Collaboration the Ultimate in Disintermediation?" *Knowledge Management,* March 2001 [http://www.destinationcrm.com/km/dcrm_km_article.asp?id=775].

Davenport, T., and Prusak, L. *Working Knowledge: How Organizations Manage What They Know.* Boston: Harvard Business School Press, 1998.

Gartner Research. "Plumtree Corporate Portal 4.5 Reaches Fruition." Sept. 2001 [http://www.plumtree.com].

Gill, P. "Closing the Loop on Transactions: MicroStrategy Transactor Helps to Turn Information into Action." *Knowledge Management,* Nov. 2000. [http://www.destinationcrm.com/km/dcrm_km_article.asp?id=449].

Mitchell, L. "Align Business Minds: MindAlign 4.0 Raises the IM Bar by Boosting Knowledge Sharing for Better Decision Making." *InfoWorld,* June 4, 2001.

Moskowitz, R. "Campus Portals Come to Higher Education." *Matrix,* June 2001.

Prewitt, E. "A Growing Body of Knowledge: What's to Know About Knowledge Management." *CIO Magazine,* Feb. 2001 [http://www.cio.com/archive/021501/et.html].

Roberts-Witt, S. L. "Making Sense of Portal Pandemonium: What's Behind the Portal Boom—and What It Means for the Future of the Enterprise." *Knowledge Management,* July 1999 [http://www.destinationcrm.com/km/dcrm_km_article.asp?id=24&ed=7%2F1%2F99].

Schreiber, G., Akkermans, H., Anjewierden, A. *Knowledge Engineering and Management: The CommonKADS Methodology.* Cambridge: MIT Press, 2000.

Wallach, S. L. "Mapping Business Landscapes: Vigil's e-Sense Provides Dynamic Answers to Business Questions." *Knowledge Management,* Dec. 2000 [http://www.destinationcrm.com/km/dcrm_km_article.asp?id=472].

Wallach, S. L. "Knowledge Workers Handle Content: Xpedio Provides the Control Users Need to Turn Content into a Knowledge Asset." *Knowledge Management,* March 2001 [http://www.destinationcrm.com/km/dcrm_km_article.asp?id=776].

ANDREEA M. SERBAN *is director of institutional assessment, research, and planning at Santa Barbara City College in Santa Barbara, California.*

JING LUAN *is chief planning and research officer at Cabrillo College in Aptos, California.*

7

*Knowledge management is more than a buzzword, it is
here to stay in some form or another because
organizations must be able to capitalize on their
cumulative knowledge in order to survive and thrive,
compete and innovate. From an institutional research
perspective, knowledge management can and has already
become the "fifth face" of our profession. Institutional
researchers have the potential to be the first generation of
knowledge managers in higher education.*

Knowledge Management: The "Fifth Face" of Institutional Research

Andreea M. Serban

In a comprehensive volume about institutional research (IR), Volkwein (1999) described our profession as having four "faces," based on the purposes and audiences we serve and the organizational role and culture in which we function. These four faces or facets include IR as information authority, IR as spin doctor, IR as policy analyst, and IR as scholar and researcher (see Figure 7.1). In a knowledge management environment, these four facets continue to exist; however, they converge into a broader, more integrated dimension—the "fifth face" of institutional research—IR as knowledge manager. Institutional research becomes a catalyst for processes that underlie the knowledge management framework—creation, capturing, and sharing of knowledge—that serve both internal and external purposes and audiences. As Volkwein (1999) notes, the four traditional dimensions of institutional research are not discrete, rather, in many cases, they coexist and overlap. The fifth dimension does not necessarily replace but it augments these traditional roles and, as the other four, is dependent on an organizational culture that promotes and supports knowledge management.

As discussed throughout this volume, institutional research has evolved as a core component of an institution's explicit knowledge base. As one of our colleagues describes it: "Institutional research is found everywhere in the higher education enterprise, from student affairs to parking. It is a mindset about data, regardless of the topic" (Milam, 2001). Institutional researchers have the potential to become the first generation of chief knowledge officers or knowledge managers in higher education or play key roles in institutional knowledge management teams.

NEW DIRECTIONS FOR INSTITUTIONAL RESEARCH, no. 113, Spring 2002 © Wiley Periodicals, Inc.

Figure 7.1. Purposes and Roles of Institutional Research

	Purposes and Audiences	
	Formative and Internal (for Improvement)	Summative and External (for Accountability)
Organizational Role and Culture		
Administrative and Institutional	To describe the institution – IR as information authority	To present the best case – IR as spin doctor
Academic and Professional	To analyze alternatives – IR as policy analyst	To supply impartial evidence of effectiveness – IR as scholar and researcher
Knowledge Management	To gather and transform data into information and knowledge; to collaborate in the creation and maintenance of an institutional official repository of data, information, and knowledge (i.e., portals); to facilitate the process of knowledge creation, capturing, and sharing. —IR as knowledge manager	

Traditional Roles (bracket spanning Administrative and Academic rows)

New Role (bracket spanning Knowledge Management row)

Source: Volkwein (1999), p. 17.

Chief Knowledge Officers and Knowledge Management Teams

The emergence and evolution of knowledge management as a needed organizational conceptual and practical operating framework in the business environment has led to the recognition that organizations could more effectively achieve it if they had a chief knowledge officer. As early as 1994, Davenport stated: "Some companies are creating room for a chief knowledge officer to manage unstructured information. Many of the companies I work with are starting to seriously address the issue of information and knowledge management. One major step they are taking is to create the post of chief knowledge officer (CKO) or an equivalent role to manage the processes of capturing, distributing, and effectively using knowledge. Organizations that have adopted this position include Hoffman-LaRoche, GE Lighting, Xerox PARC, and several consultancies, including Ernst & Young, Gemini, and McKinsey." In addition, having such a position in an organization could help send the message that knowledge is an asset to be managed and shared (Stuller, 1998).

Besides the need for capturing unstructured information, as discussed in the opening chapter, there are multiple reasons that led to the emergence of knowledge management. The same reasons support the need for the creation of CKO positions. As discussed throughout the volume, tacit knowledge is generally elusive and thus not systematically identified and managed. Many organizations now realize that they are not effectively capitalizing on the knowledge of their employees and that their long-term prosperity depends on the organizational effort to explicitly manage this knowledge and use it as a source for growth and corporate profit (Herschel and Nemati, 2001). CKOs can play many roles, ranging from serving as catalysts of the overall corporate knowledge to designing, implementing, and overseeing the institution's knowledge infrastructure to acting as liaisons between the internal and external knowledge providers (Davenport and Prusak, 1998).

Such a broad array of responsibilities requires a corresponding broad range of skills and experiences. Because knowledge management involves culture, people, and behavior as well as business processes and technology, finding the person for this job could be challenging. "The ideal CKO would be an expert in several areas, including training and development, information technology, legal and technical knowledge, and corporate information" (Flash, 2001). Some organizations recognized that in practice it is difficult to find one person who is expert in all these areas. These organizations turned to the idea of combining the leadership of a CKO with the abilities of a knowledge management team whose members can adequately address all parts of this role (Flash, 2001).

Although they are not known as knowledge management teams, cross-functional teams in higher education have served the roles outlined above, at least to some extent. However, for cross-functional teams to be effective in the development, deployment, and sustenance of an organizational knowledge management effort, the leadership of a CKO who acts primarily as an agent of change could be most beneficial.

Few higher education institutions have created a CKO position to date, although some individuals within campuses have played this role or parts of it without being designated as such. Jackson State University, a historically black institution in Jackson, Mississippi, is probably the first in the United States to have created and filled the position of associate provost for knowledge management and research, instead of creating the traditional position of director of institutional research or planning. Jackson State transformed what would be have been traditionally known as the office of institutional research into knowledge management systems and solutions [http://ccaix.jsums.edu/~jsuoaa/knowledge/knowledge.html]. Although the approach to knowledge management undertaken by Jackson State does not cover many of the processes discussed throughout this volume, it is a clear indication that in higher education, institutional researchers and planners can play a major role in advancing the knowledge management paradigm and becoming the facilitators and, in some cases, the leaders of these efforts.

Formal Training for Knowledge Management

Not unlike institutional research, knowledge management has evolved through trial and error and through the confluence of many disciplines but without a base of formal training courses, programs, or related degrees, except for training provided by some consulting firms. A few higher education institutions, however, have started offering courses and even granting degrees related to or supportive of the field, and their number is growing. Examples include the following:

- Dominican University, River Forest, Illinois, through its Center for Knowledge Management hosted by the Graduate School of Library and Information Science [http://www.dom.edu/gslis/ckm.html], offers a knowledge management certificate program designed for individuals working in the information sciences, computer sciences, or business management fields.
- George Mason University, Fairfax, Virginia, offers knowledge management courses [http://icasit.gmu.edu/km/index.htm].
- George Washington University, Washington, D.C., is teaching knowledge management to its engineering students [http://www.emse.seas.gwu.edu/emgt/new/ckm.html].
- University of Washington, Seattle, is teaching knowledge management in the context of health services [http://courses.washington.edu/~hs590a/modules/38/know38b.html].

In addition, there is a knowledge management certification board [http://www.kmcertification.org], whose mission is to set professional standards and provide certification for knowledge management professionals. "The Certified Knowledge Manager™ (CKM) is exposed to two areas of study: General Knowledge Management and Knowledge Environment Engineering" [eknowledgecenter.com/certificationcourses/index.htm].

Benefits and Challenges of Knowledge Management

The chapters in this volume explore the theoretical and practical aspects of knowledge management and provide examples of how knowledge management processes, technologies, products, and models are applied in and can benefit higher education, in general, and institutional research, in particular.

Benefits. There are clear advantages of implementing knowledge management frameworks and processes, summarized as follows:

Access to and Sharing of Knowledge. The advances in technology discussed and exemplified throughout the volume allow higher education institutions to create knowledge management infrastructures, which facilitate rapid access to and sharing of knowledge throughout the organization. The advent of portal technology, discussed in Chapter Three, for example, has changed dramatically the way information and knowledge are created, captured, accessed, and shared. Overall, the host of technologies that support knowledge management, discussed in Chapter Six, have made virtual organizations a reality.

Customer Responsiveness. A well-thought-out and implemented knowledge management framework can improve dramatically the ability of higher education institutions to respond to and interact with its many different customers from prospective students and their parents to alumni and vendors. As discussed in Chapter Four, customer relationship management (CRM), in conjunction with a portal environment, can provide effective personalized customer service.

Better Understanding of the Organization and Its Customers. Techniques such as data mining provide institutional researchers with a powerful way for understanding data residing in various organizational databases and data warehouses by discovering patterns and making predictions that can help craft better strategies for improving student access and success, as well as institutional effectiveness in general. In addition, document and content management can enhance the overall ability of any employee to better understand the functions, operations, and processes within an organization through direct access to the knowledge embedded in many policies, procedures, and other documents.

Operational Efficiencies and Decentralization of Functions. A comprehensive knowledge management infrastructure can improve operational efficiency by enhancing collaboration between individuals and organizational units and by enabling employees to conduct operations that in the past required the expertise of a centralized department such as the Web development group or Web master of an institution. For example, as discussed in Chapter Three, the Web development and maintenance capabilities embedded within portal products allow employees to post and change documents on the Web without experience in html coding. As a result, the Web presence of departments could be improved through easy updating of the materials posted. While many institutional researchers have become conversant in Web related software packages, such functionality allows them to take full advantage of the Web without the need to spend extensive amounts of time in Web development per se.

Challenges. The following challenges may also be encountered in implementing knowledge management frameworks and processes.

Strategy. As Manville and Foote (1996) noted, knowledge management is meaningless unless an organization has a clear sense of direction and strategy, or as they describe it: "If a company does not have its fundamentals in place, all the corporate learning, information technology, or knowledge databases are mere costly diversions" (p. 66).

Tacit Knowledge and Organizational Cultures. Although a stated purpose of knowledge management is to capitalize on the tacit knowledge of employees, this is more difficult to achieve in practice than to assert in theory. As underscored throughout the volume, whereas the importance of explicit knowledge should not be undermined, it is the tacit knowledge that often drives innovation within organizations. "There is a corollary to the importance of tacit knowledge: people will not willingly share it with coworkers if their workplace culture does not support learning, cooperation, and openness" (Manville and Foote, 1996, p. 66).

Skills and Expertise. Although many products and technologies are fairly easy to use once implemented, this is rarely the case during the installation, set-up, and deployment phase. Many of these products are very complex and difficult to set up, requiring staff with extensive technical knowledge and sophistication. In most cases, to take full advantage of the functionality and capabilities that some of the knowledge management processes and technologies offer, employees need various degrees of training.

Cost. The implementation of knowledge management infrastructures and processes is costly in terms of both human and financial resources. The discussion related to workflow in Chapter Three, for example, indicates that substantial time and effort go into the examination, evaluation, and change, when needed, of business processes that are the base for the adoption of an automated workflow model. Generally, products supporting various knowledge management processes are fairly expensive and might be prohibitive for smaller institutions with low budgets and very limited discretionary resources.

Conclusion

Although specific approaches to knowledge management vary from one organization to another, several themes emerge. Knowledge management requires a shift in organizational culture and a commitment at all organizational levels to make it work. A strong technological infrastructure provides the tools needed for ensuring the success of knowledge management efforts. However, technology alone will do little to achieve a sustained and comprehensive knowledge management framework that permeates the entire organization. Beyond the use of technology, knowledge management requires a new approach to tying data, information, and knowledge that facilitates understanding and promotes action.

The constant change in organizational environments has increased the need to capitalize on organizational knowledge in order to stay competitive and become innovative. We learn from what people are doing. Knowledge management strives to effectively record and disseminate peoples' tacit and explicit knowledge so that others can learn and use it.

There is, however, some degree of skepticism about knowledge management mainly because it is still a fairly new field, especially in higher education. One of the areas in need of development is the measurement of knowledge management effectiveness. These measures should answer questions such as, How does knowledge management work for an organization? What is the value added by knowledge management processes and products?

Knowledge management is more than a buzzword. It is here to stay because its fundamental premise of harnessing organizational knowledge is at the core of what most twenty-first-century organizations need to survive and thrive. "The newly empowered knowledge worker will live in a world of immense choice that may often imply living with immense risks and immense returns. The feeling will be simultaneously exhilarating and unnerving: the joy of freedom to choose blended with the apprehension of making one's own choices and having to live with them" (Malhotra, 2000).

References

Davenport, T. "Coming Soon: The CKO." *Techweb,* Sept. 1994.

Davenport, T., and Prusak, L. *Working Knowledge.* Boston: Harvard Business School, 1998.

Flash, C. "Who Is the CKO?" *Knowledge Management,* May 2001.

Herschel, R. T., and Nemati, H. "Chief Knowledge Officers: Managing Knowledge for Organizational Effectiveness." In Y. Malhotra (ed.), *Knowledge Management and Business Model Innovation.* Hershey, Pa.: Idea Group Publishing, 2001.

Malhotra, Y. "What Is the Big Idea? Knowledge and Its Future." *The Executive Report on Knowledge, Technology and Performance.* Knowledge Inc., The Millennium Issue, January 2000, 5(1). Austin, Tex.: Quantum Enterprises. [http://www.knowledgeinc.com].

Manville, B., and Foote, N. "Strategy as if Knowledge Mattered." *FastCompany,* April 1996, 2, 66.

Milam, J. H. "Knowledge Management: A Revolution Waiting for IR." Paper presented at the AIR Annual Forum, Long Beach, Calif., June 1–4, 2001.

Stuller, J. "Chief of Corporate Smarts." *Training,* 1998, 35(4), 28–37.

Volkwein, J. F. "The Four Faces of Institutional Research." *What Is Institutional Research All About? A Critical and Comprehensive Assessment of the Profession.* New Directions for Institutional Research, no. 104. San Francisco: Jossey Bass, 1999.

ANDREEA M. SERBAN is director of institutional assessment, research, and planning at Santa Barbara City College in Santa Barbara, California.

INDEX

Back Issue/Subscription Order Form

Copy or detach and send to:

Jossey-Bass, A Wiley Company, 989 Market Street, San Francisco CA 94103-1741

Call or fax toll-free: Phone 888-378-2537 6:30AM – 3PM PST; Fax 415-951-8553

Back Issues: Please send me the following issues at $27 each
(Important: please include series initials and issue number, such as IR115)

1. IR_____

_____

_____

$ _____ Total for single issues

$ _____ SHIPPING CHARGES: SURFACE   Domestic Canadian

		Domestic	Canadian
	First Item	$5.00	$6.00
	Each Add'l Item	$3.00	$1.50

For next-day and second-day delivery rates, call the number listed above.

Subscriptions Please ❑ start ❑ renew my subscription to *New Directions for Institutional Research* for the year 2_____at the following rate:

U.S.	❑ Individual $65	❑ Institutional $125
Canada	❑ Individual $65	❑ Institutional $165
All Others	❑ Individual $89	❑ Institutional $199

$ _____ Total single issues and subscriptions (Add appropriate sales tax for your state for single issue orders. No sales tax for U.S. subscriptions. Canadian residents, add GST for subscriptions and single issues.)

❑Payment enclosed (U.S. check or money order only)

❑VISA ❑ MC ❑ AmEx ❑ Discover Card #_____ Exp. Date _____

Signature _____ Day Phone _____

❑ Bill Me (U.S. institutional orders only. Purchase order required.)

Purchase order # _____

Federal Tax ID13559302   **GST 89102 8052**

Name _____

Address _____

_____

Phone _____ E-mail _____

For more information about Jossey-Bass, visit our Web site at www.josseybass.com

PROMOTION CODE ND3

United States Postal Service

Statement of Ownership, Management, and Circulation

1. Publication Title New Directions for Institutional Research	2. Publication Number 0 2 7 1 _ 0 5 7 9	3. Filing Date 9/28/01

4. Issue Frequency Quarterly	5. Number of Issues Published Annually 4	6. Annual Subscription Price $65.00 Individua $125.00 Instituti

7. Complete Mailing Address of Known Office of Publication *(Not printer) (Street, city, county, state, and ZIP+4)* 989 Market St San Francisco, CA 94103 (San Francisco County)	Contact Person Joe Schuman
	Telephone 415-782-3232

8. Complete Mailing Address of Headquarters or General Business Office of Publisher *(Not printer)*

Same as Above

9. Full Names and Complete Mailing Addresses of Publisher, Editor, and Managing Editor *(Do not leave blank)*

Publisher *(Name and complete mailing address)*

Jossey-Bass, A Wiley Company

Editor *(Name and complete mailing address)*   J. Fredericks Volkwein
Pennsylvania State University
403 South Allen Street, STE 104
University Park, PA 16801-5252

Managing Editor *(Name and complete mailing address)*

None

10. Owner *(Do not leave blank. If the publication is owned by a corporation, give the name and address of the corporation immediately followed by the names and addresses of all stockholders owning or holding 1 percent or more of the total amount of stock. If not owned by a corporation, give the names and addresses of the individual owners. If owned by a partnership or other unincorporated firm, give its name and address as well as those of each individual owner. If the publication is published by a nonprofit organization, give its name and address.)*

Full Name	Complete Mailing Address
John Wiley & Sons, Inc	605 Third Avenue New York, NY 10158-0012

11. Known Bondholders, Mortgagees, and Other Security Holders Owning or Holding 1 Percent or More of Total Amount of Bonds, Mortgages, or Other Securities. If none, check box ➤ ☐ None

Full Name	Complete Mailing Address
Same as above	Same as Above

12. Tax Status *(For completion by nonprofit organizations authorized to mail at nonprofit rates) (Check one)*
The purpose, function, and nonprofit status of this organization and the exempt status for federal income tax purposes:
☐ Has Not Changed During Preceding 12 Months
☐ Has Changed During Preceding 12 Months *(Publisher must submit explanation of change with this statement)*

PS Form **3526**, October 1999   *(See Instructions on Reverse)*

13. Publication Title			14. Issue Date for Circulation Data Below	
New Directions for Institutional Research			Summer 2001	

15 Extent and Nature of Circulation			Average No. Copies Each Issue During Preceding 12 Months	No. Copies of Single Issue Published Nearest to Filing Date
a. Total Number of Copies (Net press run)			1,826	1,660
b. Paid and/or Requested Circulation	(1)	Paid/Requested Outside-County Mail Subscriptions Stated on Form 3541. (Include advertiser's proof and exchange copies)	695	663
	(2)	Paid In-County Subscriptions Stated on Form 3541 (Include advertiser's proof and exchange copies)	0	0
	(3)	Sales Through Dealers and Carriers, Street Vendors, Counter Sales, and Other Non-USPS Paid Distribution	131	106
	(4)	Other Classes Mailed Through the USPS	0	0
c. Total Paid and/or Requested Circulation [Sum of 15b. (1), (2),(3),and (4)] ▶			826	769
d. Free Distribution by Mail (Samples, complimentary, and other free)	(1)	Outside-County as Stated on Form 3541	0	0
	(2)	In-County as Stated on Form 3541	0	0
	(3)	Other Classes Mailed Through the USPS	1	1
e. Free Distribution Outside the Mail (Carriers or other means)			64	57
f. Total Free Distribution (Sum of 15d. and 15e.) ▶			65	58
g. Total Distribution (Sum of 15c. and 15f) ▶			891	827
h. Copies not Distributed			935	833
i. Total (Sum of 15g. and h.) ▶			1,826	1,660
j. Percent Paid and/or Requested Circulation (15c. divided by 15g. times 100)			92%	93%

16 Publication of Statement of Ownership

☒ Publication required. Will be printed in the __Winter 2001__ issue of this publication. ☐ Publication not required.

17. Signature and Title of Editor, Publisher, Business Manager, or Owner Susan E. Lewis Vice President & Publisher - Periodicals	Date 9/28/01

I certify that all information furnished on this form is true and complete. I understand that anyone who furnishes false or misleading information on this form or who omits material or information requested on the form may be subject to criminal sanctions (including fines and imprisonment) and/or civil sanctions (including civil penalties).

Instructions to Publishers

1. Complete and file one copy of this form with your postmaster annually on or before October 1. Keep a copy of the completed form for your records.

2. In cases where the stockholder or security holder is a trustee, include in items 10 and 11 the name of the person or corporation for whom the trustee is acting. Also include the names and addresses of individuals who are stockholders who own or hold 1 percent or more of the total amount of bonds, mortgages, or other securities of the publishing corporation: In item 11, if none, check the box. Use blank sheets if more space is required.

3. Be sure to furnish all circulation information called for in item 15. Free circulation must be shown in items 15d, e, and f.

4. Item 15h., Copies not Distributed, must include (1) newsstand copies originally stated on Form 3541, and returned to the publisher, (2) estimated returns from news agents, and (3), copies for office use, leftovers, spoiled, and all other copies not distributed.

5. If the publication had Periodicals authorization as a general or requester publication, this Statement of Ownership, Management, and Circulation must be published; it must be printed in any issue in October or, if the publication is not published during October, the first issue printed after October.

6. In item 16, indicate the date of the issue in which this Statement of Ownership will be published.

7. Item 17 must be signed.

Failure to file or publish a statement of ownership may lead to suspension of Periodicals authorization.

PS Form 3526, October 1999 (Reverse)

student development theory in formulating research questions, the value of qualitative methods it employs, and the potential contribution it can make to institutional decision making.
ISBN: 0-7879-5727-5

IR107   **Understanding the College Choice of Disadvantaged Students**
Alberto F. Cabrera, Steven M. La Nasa
Examines the college-choice decision of minority and disadvantaged students and suggests avenues to help promote access and improve participation. Explores the influence of family and high school variables as well as racial and ethnic differences on college-choice.
ISBN: 0-7879-5439-X

IR106   **Analyzing Costs in Higher Education: What Institutional Researchers Need to Know**
Michael F. Middaugh
Presents both the conceptual and practical information that will give researchers solid grounding in selecting the best approach to cost analysis. Offers an overview of cost studies covering basic issues and beyond, from a review of definitions of expenditure categories and rules of financial reporting to a discussion of a recent congressionally mandated study of higher education costs.
ISBN: 0-7879-5437-3

IR105   **What Contributes to Job Satisfaction Among Faculty and Staff**
Linda Serra Hagedorn
Argues that positive outcomes for the entire campus can only be achieved within an environment that considers the satisfaction of all of those employed in the academy. Examines various jobs within the campus community—including classified staff and student affairs administrators as well as faculty—and suggests factors that will promote job satisfaction.
ISBN: 0-7879-5438-1

IR104   **What Is Institutional Research All About? A Critical and Comprehensive Assessment of the Profession**
J. Fredericks Volkwein
Chapters explore the role IR plays in improving an institution's ability to learn, review organizational behavior theories that shed light on the researcher's relationship with the institution, and discuss the three tiers of organizational intelligence that make up IR—technical/analytical, contextual, and issues intelligence.
ISBN: 0-7879-1406-1

IR103   **How Technology Is Changing Institutional Research**
Liz Sanders
Illustrates how to streamline office functions through the use of new technologies, assesses the impact of distance learning on faculty workload and student learning, and responds to the new opportunities and problems posed by expanding information access.
ISBN: 0-7879-5240-0

IR102   **Information Technology in Higher Education: Assessing Its Impact and Planning for the Future**
Richard N. Katz, Julia A. Rudy
Provides campus leaders, institutional researchers, and information technologists much-needed guidance for determining how IT investments

should be made, measured, and assessed. Offers practical, effective models for integrating IT planning into institutional planning and goals, assessing the impact of IT investments on teaching, learning, and administrative operations, and promoting efficient information management practices.
ISBN: 0-7879-1409-6

IR101   **A New Era of Alumni Research: Improving Institutional Performance and Better Serving Alumni**
Joseph Pettit, Larry L. Litten
Drawing from information generated by mail and telephone surveys, focus groups, and institutional data analysis, the authors examine various facets of an institution's relationship with alumni—including fundraising from alumni, services for alumni, and occupational and other outcomes of college.
ISBN: 0-7879-1407-X

IR100   **Using Teams in Higher Education: Cultural Foundations for Productive Change**
Susan H. Frost
Using research and practice from higher education, where teams are used with varying degrees of effectiveness, and from business, where teams are linked to survival, this issue addresses questions of culture, especially as they can affect significant aspects of teamwork. Explores the theory and practice related to different types of teams and the dynamics that influence success.
ISBN: 0-7879-1415-0

IR99   **Quality Assurance in Higher Education: An International Perspective**
Gerald H. Gaither
Offers an international set of resources—including Web sites and other electronic resources—to assist practitioners in achieving the goals of their own quality assurance frameworks.
ISBN: 0-7879-4740-7

IR98   **Campus Climate: Understanding the Critical Components of Today's Colleges and Universities**
Karen W. Bauer
Provides guidelines for effective assessment of today's diverse campus populations, highlighting key diversity issues that affect women, racial and ethnic minorities; and lesbian, gay, bisexual, transgender, and disabled students.
ISBN: 0-78791416-9

IR97   **Performance Funding for Public Higher Education: Fad or Trend?**
Joseph C. Burke, Andreea M. Serban
Examines the conflicts and issues raised by performance funding as well as the similarities and differences in state programs. Discusses the information gathered and lessons learned from a national study of performance funding supported by The Pew Charitable Trusts.
ISBN: 0-7879-1417-7

IR96   **Preventing Lawsuits: The Role of Institutional Research**
Larry G. Jones
Examines what institutions and institutional researchers might do to keep themselves out of court, although contributors also suggest how institutional research pertains when institutions do end up in court. Discusses how preventive law—the efforts of attorneys and clients to minimize legal risks—may be the most appropriate construct for meeting the needs of institutions.
ISBN: 0-7879-9876-1

IR95   **Researching Student Aid: Creating an Action Agenda**
        Richard A. Voorhees
        Provides researchers with the tools they need to make sense of the complex
        interplay of politics, students, and institutions that constitute our current
        system of student aid. Reports of three empirical studies within this issue
        provide concrete examples of the types of research institutional researchers can
        execute on behalf of their campuses.
        ISBN: 0-7879-9875-3

IR94   **Mobilizing for Transformation: How Campuses Are Preparing for the
        Knowledge Age**
        Donald M. Norris, James L. Morrison
        Provides practical insight and guidance to campus leaders who are attempting
        to accelerate the transformation of their campuses to meet the challenges and
        opportunities of the Knowledge Age. This insight is drawn from case studies
        and vignettes from nearly twenty campuses that have succeeded in leveraging
        the forces of transformation on their campuses.
        ISBN: 0-7879-9851-6

IR93   **Forecasting and Managing Enrollment and Revenue: An Overview of
        Current Trends, Issues, and Methods**
        Daniel T. Layzell
        Examines demographic, economic, and financial trends affecting enrollment
        and revenue management and forecasting in higher education, practical
        examples and issues in enrollment and revenue management and forecasting
        (for both public and private institutions), current methods and techniques of
        enrollment and revenue forecasting in higher education, and an evaluation of
        lessons learned in these areas.
        ISBN: 0-7879-9850-8

IR92   **Assessing Graduate and Professional Education: Current Realities, Future
        Prospects**
        Jennifer Grant Haworth
        Despite its burgeoning popularity, the assessment movement has focused
        largely on undergraduate education, leaving institutional researchers,
        administrators, and faculty with scant information on methods for conducting
        assessments of graduate and professional education and a dearth of the results
        of such assessments.
        ISBN: 0-7879-9899-0

IR91   **Campus Fact Books: Keeping Pace with New Institutional Needs and
        Challenges**
        Larry G. Jones
        Explores ways in which the campus fact book can remain and grow as a
        significant institutional research report, both in light of new reporting demands
        and opportunities and in response to new and increased demands and uses for
        institutional data and information from and by internal and external
        constituencies.
        ISBN: 0-7879-9900-8

IR90   **Faculty Teaching and Research: Is There a Conflict?**
        John M. Braxton
        Examines empirical evidence concerning the relationship between faculty
        research activity and such facets of their teaching as classroom performance,
        teaching preparations, the influence of teaching behaviors on student learning,
        faculty goals for undergraduate education, faculty attitudes and behaviors

concerning their interactions with students, pedagogical practices, course assessment activities, norms delineating inappropriate teaching behaviors, and adherence to good teaching practices.
ISBN: 0-7879-9898-2

IR88　**Evaluating and Responding to College Guidebooks and Rankings**
R. Dan Walleri, Marsha K. Moss
Explores issues surrounding college guidebooks and ratings. The background and development of these publications are traced, followed by discussion of major issues and perspectives—consumer use of the publications, validity of ratings, and the institutional burden of supplying the needed information.
ISBN: 0-7879-9944-X

IR87　**Student Tracking: New Techniques, New Demands**
Peter T. Ewell
Describes important changes in the requirements for student tracking data bases and examines the expanding technical possibilities provided by statewide administrative data bases and by the availability of greatly enhanced data-manipulation and statistical tools for constructing and analyzing longitudinal data files.
ISBN: 0-7879-9943-1

IR86　**Using Academic Program Review**
Robert J. Barak, Lisa A. Mets
Provides planners and institutional researchers with information on the uses of program review results in colleges and universities.
ISBN: 0-7879-9920-2

IR85　**Preparing for the Information Needs of the Twenty-First Century**
Timothy R. Sanford
Offers reference points for the institutional researcher and planner as postsecondary education plunges into the twenty-first century. Charts possible ways the world of higher education may evolve in the next ten to fifteen years.
ISBN: 0-7879-9919-9

IR84　**Providing Useful Information for Deans and Department Chairs**
Mary K. Kinnick
Argues that institutional researchers need to give more attention to deans and department chairs and suggests methods for providing them with the information that will help them to understand changing student needs; facilitate and assess student learning; assess and understand faculty culture; and redefine, assign, and assess faculty work.
ISBN: 0-7879-9989-X

IR83　**Analyzing Faculty Workload**
Jon F. Wergin
Explores how the public discourse about faculty work might be improved and suggests how colleges and universities might document that work in a fashion that not only more faithfully describes what faculty do but also allows for reports that are more comprehensive and useful.
ISBN: 0-7879-9988-1

IR82　**Using Performance Indicators to Guide Strategic Decision Making**
Victor M. H. Borden, Trudy W. Banta
The goal of this issue is threefold: to provide the reader with an understanding of what has led to the current popularity of indicator systems; to illustrate

several possible methods for developing performance indicators; and to synthesize theory and practice into a formulation for a proactive, institution-based approach to indicator development.
ISBN: 0-7879-9964-4

IR78   **Pursuit of Quality in Higher Education: Case Studies in Total Quality Management**
Deborah J. Teeter, G. Gregory Lozier
Provides valuable insights into the experiences of colleges and universities that are applying the principles of Total Quality Management (TQM) to higher education. Presents different aspects of TQM regarding issues of organization, training, use of tools or methodologies, the language of TQM, or the challenges in transforming organizational cultures.
ISBN: 1-55542-693-X

IR66   **Organizing Effective Institutional Research Offices**
Jennifer B. Presley
Designed to assist both those who are establishing an institutional research function for the first time and those who are invigorating an existing unit. Provides major guidelines for how to approach tasks and avoid major pitfalls.
ISBN: 1-55542-829-0

IR61   **Planning and Managing Higher Education Facilities**
Harvey H. Kaiser
Provides information on facilities management for institutional researchers, with theories and application covering a range of topics from a global perspective to specific issues.
ISBN: 1-55542-868-1

IR55   **Managing Information in Higher Education**
E. Michael Staman
Describes many of the key elements in the development of an information management program and the policies and procedures that must be in place if the program is to be successful and sustainable over time.
ISBN: 1-55542-947-5